Waking Up

A Week Inside a Zen Monastery

Jack Maguire

Foreword by John Daido Loori, Roshi

Walking Together, Finding the Way

SKYLIGHT PATHS PUBLISHING
WOODSTOCK, VERMONT

Waking Up:
A Week Inside a Zen Monastery

© 2000 by SkyLight Paths Publishing

Photographs courtesy the Zen Mountain Monastery Archive.

Library of Congress Cataloging-in-Publication Data
Maguire, Jack, 1945–
   Waking up : a week inside a Zen monastery / Jack Maguire ; foreword by
     John Daido Loori.
        p.   cm.
   Includes bibliographical references.
   ISBN 1-893361-13-6
     1. Monastic and religious life (Zen Buddhism)—United States. I. Title.
   BQ9294.4. U6 M34 2000
   294.3'927—dc21   00-010977

10 9 8 7 6 5 4 3 2 1

Manufactured in the United States of America
Jacket design by Bronwen Battaglia
Text design by Chelsea Cloeter

SkyLight Paths, "Walking Together, Finding the Way" and colophon are trademarks of LongHill Partners, Inc., registered in the U.S. Patent and Trademark Office.

Walking Together, Finding the Way
Published by SkyLight Paths Publishing
A Division of LongHill Partners, Inc.
Sunset Farm Offices, Route 4, P.O. Box 237
Woodstock, VT 05091
Tel: (802) 457 4000   Fax: (802) 457 4004
www.skylightpaths.com

In tribute to the many ways that each of them has helped save my life, this book is dedicated to my teachers at Zen Mountain Monastery: John Daido Loori, Roshi; Bonnie Myotai Treace, Sensei; and Geoffrey Shugen Arnold, Sensei.

Contents

Acknowledgments

Every day I am thankful for the example and support of the community at Zen Mountain Monastery. I am especially grateful to the people who, with much generosity and trust, put their own experiences into words for this book. Some of these individuals have enriched my life for a long time. Others, among them newcomers to the monastery, I first met in the context of asking for an interview: I let my Zen-stoked intuition lead me to them, and their thoughtful responses validated its worth. I only wish that time and space had permitted me to include in these pages personal testimony from the many other people I know at the monastery whose insights I value.

I am obliged to Jon Sweeney, associate publisher at SkyLight Paths Publishing, for his creative work in putting this project together, and to Dave O'Neal, development editor, for his expert editorial guidance.

I also thank Konrad Ryushin Marchaj, managing editor of Dharma Communications, for granting me permission to quote from various issues of the *Mountain Record*, Zen Mountain Monastery's quarterly journal, and to reprint certain chants and precepts that appear in the

Zen Mountain Monastery Liturgy Manual (both the journal and the manual can be ordered through Dharma Communications: see appendix A: "Zen Mountain Monastery" under New York). In addition, I appreciate his help in selecting and transferring the photographs that appear in this book, all of which belong to the monastery's archives.

Finally, I offer deep gratitude to my teacher, John Daido Loori, Roshi, abbot of Zen Mountain Monastery, for writing the foreword to this book. His words and deeds are a constant source of inspiration to me and countless other sentient beings.

Foreword

Twenty-five centuries ago in northern India, near what is now Nepal, Siddhartha Gautama, a young prince of the kingdom of the Shakyas, came face to face with the ultimate question of human existence: Why is there suffering, sickness, old age, and death? At the age of twenty-nine, Siddhartha left his family and entered this question. He followed a group of ascetics who undertook several practices such as fasting and sleep deprivation.

It is said that Siddhartha was very skilled in these rigorous practices and that he followed them faithfully, but after a while he reached a point where his body became so emaciated and weakened that he couldn't go on any more. He said to himself, "I am no closer to the answers to my question than I was at the beginning." He decided to abandon the way of the ascetic and instead nourished and rested his body until his strength returned. His fellow ascetics were appalled and deserted Siddhartha, who continued to wander alone through the forest, probably "the loneliest figure in history, searching for light," as one historian called him. Left to himself, Siddhartha once again vowed not to rest until he had found the answers he was searching for, and when he came across the *bodhi* tree, he sat down under it and resolutely began a single-minded meditation.

On the third morning under the bodhi tree, at the break of day, this young man—afterward called the Buddha (in Sanskrit, "the awakened one")—saw the morning star and immediately experienced a great enlightenment. He exclaimed, "Isn't it wonderful? Isn't it marvelous? All sentient beings, this great earth, and I have at once entered the Way." He meant that all sentient beings, this great earth, and he himself were perfect and complete, lacking nothing. Sitting under the bodhi tree he discovered that he already had what he was seeking. When others saw him, they could see that some kind of transformation had taken place in him, so they asked him to teach what he had realized. At first he refused. He knew there wasn't anything he could teach them; there wasn't anything they could attain, since, like him, they were already perfect and complete. His old ascetic friends begged him, and finally he relented and delivered his first teaching to a small group at a place called Deer Park in what is now Sarnath, India.

In his first teaching the Buddha taught the four wisdoms (also known as the four noble truths). The first wisdom is the wisdom of suffering. The Buddha said, "Life is suffering (*duhkha*)." In this teaching he included all forms of suffering: physical, mental, and emotional. But he was also referring to that which we might not necessarily regard as suffering, such as higher states of meditation, blissful states that, because of their impermanent nature, still cause us pain when we cling to them.

The second wisdom is the cause of suffering, which the Buddha described as thirst or desire. It arises out of the notion that there exists a self separate and distinct from everything else. We think that who we are is this bag of skin and that everything encapsulated within it is me and everything outside of it is the rest of the world. We constantly crave for what we think we lack, and so we suffer.

In the third wisdom the Buddha said that it is possible to put an end to suffering, and the fourth wisdom, called the eightfold path, is the set of practices that leads to the cessation of suffering. These are: right understanding, right thought, right speech, right action, right livelihood, right effort, right mindfulness, and right concentration.

After having taught these four wisdoms, the Buddha spent the next forty-five years elaborating on these basic teachings. He taught in different ways in accord with the circumstances he encountered, using what we call skillful means (*upaya*). He addressed numerous assemblies and taught people from all walks of life. On one occasion the Buddha stood before an assembly of thousands on Vulture Peak. Everyone waited eagerly for his teachings, but instead of a long discourse of explanations or proclamations, the Buddha simply held up a flower and twirled it. Only one of his disciples, Mahakashyapa—or Kasho, as he is also known—recognized his master's teaching. The Buddha then said, "I have the all-pervading dharma, the exquisite teaching of formless form. It is not transmitted through words and letters. It is now in the hands of Mahakashyapa."

According to the Zen tradition, this event marked the first transmission of the teaching mind to mind, from teacher to disciple. It set in motion a process that has continued through successive generations for twenty-five hundred years down to the present. And yet, the question begging to be asked is: What exactly is transmitted? If the Buddha's realization was that we are all perfect and complete, lacking nothing, then what is there to teach?

Today the Buddha-dharma is alive here in the West. There are centers and monasteries all over the country, with teachers and students engaging the Buddha's centuries-old teaching in a way that is relevant to modern-day practitioners facing real challenges. One of the most vital aspects of Zen is its ability to take the shape of the container that holds it. Here at Zen Mountain Monastery, the Buddha's eightfold path is manifested as the Eight Gates of Zen, a comprehensive training matrix designed to help students clarify the nature of the self.

At the heart of the Eight Gates is *zazen,* seated meditation. Nowadays zazen tends to be lumped together with all sorts of meditation forms, from yoga to tantra to stress control, and everything in between. But zazen is a very specific practice. Strictly speaking, it is not meditation. It is not contemplation, introspection, quieting the mind, focusing the mind, mindfulness, or mindlessness. It is not about visualization, mantras, or mudras. It is not about sitting cross-legged on a cushion. The zazen that I am referring to is a way of using our minds and of living our lives, and of doing it with other people. Zazen is the core, the digestive process of Zen practice. It is the device that pushes the edges of the envelope of the self.

The second gate is the teacher-student relationship. All the schools of Buddhism have teachers of one kind or another, but in Zen the teacher-student relationship is pivotal, because the transmission of the Buddha-dharma can only take place mind to mind, from teacher to disciple. During periods of zazen, students meet one to one with the teacher in the *dokusan* (interview) room, bringing questions that arise from their practice or presenting their understanding of a particular koan. Koans are paradoxical questions that meditators sit with, such as "You know the sound of two hands clapping; what is the sound of one hand clapping? Don't tell me, show me." This question is no different from the questions "What is truth?" "What is life?" "What is death?" "What is God?" "Who am I?" These questions all address the ultimate nature of reality, and they are an integral part of the dialogue between teacher and student.

Liturgy is the third gate of training, and it is one that often presents a paradox to Western practitioners, simply because Buddhism is nontheistic. The Buddha is not a god and liturgy is not about worship, yet in a Zen service there is an altar and an officiant, and people chant together and bow to a Buddha figure. What is going on? It is helpful to keep in mind that liturgy is always an expression of the common experience of a religion's adherents. In Buddhism, liturgy helps to express, by making visible, the unity of all things.

The fourth gate is right action, the precepts, which are the moral and ethical teachings of Zen. Here, as in liturgy, the responsibility for following the precepts lies solely with each practitioner, since there is no god or divine figure to determine right from wrong.

The fifth gate is called art practice, the study of how zazen forms the creative process. There is a very special group of arts that has evolved over the centuries called the arts of Zen, sometimes also called the artless arts of Zen. These arts came out of the monasteries of Sung dynasty China and the Kamakura period of Japan, and they are quite distinct from other arts that existed at those times, including the sacred arts of Buddhism. They are not based on iconography. They are not intended as religious ornaments or as records of spiritual experience. Instead they aim to express the total intimacy between artist and subject through a particularly unique aesthetic.

Body practice is the sixth of the Eight Gates. More than just physical exercise, body practice addresses the question of how to use the body—not to transcend or deny it, as is the aim in other religions, but to realize the true nature of the self. The principles of body practice are almost as old as Buddhism itself. They deal with energy (*ki*) and its function in the body as well as its relationship to healing and developing both the external musculature and the internal organs. In its most fundamental form, body practice is the whole body-and-mind engagement of each and every activity.

The seventh gate of training is academic study. America is not a Buddhist country; we do not have a Buddhist culture. Most of the information we have about Buddhism comes from articles in popular magazines or from movies. With the media as the main source of our education regarding Buddhism, it is critical that we as Westerners take up academic study. In this way, Buddhism's history, philosophy, and principles are woven together with actual practice. Only then can the full picture of this twenty-five-hundred-year-old tradition be revealed to us.

Finally, there is work practice, the eighth and most difficult aspect of Zen training. Most of our lives are spent working, so the challenge for us is how to take our practice out of the context of the monastery and bring it into the world. In its most basic form, work is just physical labor, but even the most menial task can be the manifestation of right livelihood, the kind of work that is done with single-minded concentration, with respect of tools and workspace. It is work that nourishes not only you but also your coworkers, the people you serve, and the people who serve you. Until our practice can function in everything that we do, it is not real Zen practice.

These gates of training are designed to help the practitioner get in touch with the free, unconditioned nature of the self. Generally, we are as programmed as any computer. There is no way to avoid it. From the moment we are born we become conditioned by our culture, our parents, our teachers, our education, our peers. We learn from childhood to respond to circumstances in a particular way, basing our sense of ourselves on the notions of this culture. Society tells us through infomercials and advertisements what to think and feel, what is good and not good. In direct opposition is the process of practice, which slowly shows us how to examine that conditioning, layer by layer, working our way through it to the ground of being, because buried under all these layers is a person, perfect and complete, lacking nothing. This person is none other than a buddha.

Realizing this original perfection transforms our way of perceiving ourselves and the universe. But realization is not enough. The next step is to actualize what we have seen, bringing our understanding into everything that we do: the way we drive a car, raise a child, relate to other people, maintain a relationship, grow a garden.

To realize the ground of being is wisdom (in Sanskrit, *prajna*). Wisdom is the realization of the identity of self and other. When we realize that the two are not separate, suddenly it becomes clear that the whole universe is nothing but the self, and that what happens in the farthest reaches of space happens to me personally. The famine in Mozambique affects me directly. The decimation of the Amazon forest hurts me. Once we have realized this truth, there is no way we can avoid taking responsibility for the whole catastrophe. This is where the actualization of wisdom comes into being in the form of compassion (*karuna*). By taking responsibility for the whole universe, we empower ourselves to act on behalf of its well-being, because it is *our* well-being. Instead of playing the victim and blaming someone else for our pain, we take responsibility and we do something about it. Instead of saying, "He made me angry," we realize that only we can make ourselves angry. Then we become empowered to do something about anger. Seen from this perspective, only I can transform the world. This means each one of us.

The questions we face today are the same questions of twenty-five hundred years ago, and the process for resolving these questions remains as relevant in the twenty-first century as it was in the time of the Buddha. As Zen practitioners very quickly discover, question and answer arise from the exact same place. Because so much of Zen Buddhism is based on direct experience, this process of exploration is very difficult to explain to someone without previous experience of it. This book is a courageous attempt to describe the indescribable.

Jack Hosho Maguire has skillfully managed to lay out not only the broad aspects of Zen practice but also the many subtleties that are often the key points of training. Jack's abilities as a writer and storyteller present a doorway to the ineffable through which he shares with the reader his years of experience as a dedicated Zen practitioner.

A noted historian once said that hundreds of years from now, when we look back at the twentieth century, the most significant event of the period will not be technological advancement, the invention of computers, the utilization of cyberspace, or space travel, but rather something that was hardly noticed at the time of its inception: the movement of Buddhism from East to West.

Now we stand at the beginning of the twenty-first century. The Buddha's flower has traveled from continent to continent across the great earth to find itself on these shores. It is now in the hands of Western practitioners—*our* hands. Please do not let it go unnoticed.

> *Appearing without form*
> *responding in accord with the imperative.*
> *The fragrance of the ancient flower held up*
> *fills the universe, existing right here now.*

John Daido Loori
Tremper Mountain

Waking Up

Introduction

Zen is simply a voice crying, "Wake up! Wake up!"
—MAHA STHAVIRA SANGHARAKSHITA

In Zen Buddhism, *waking up* means shaking off the sleep of everyday consciousness to experience a more enlightened, more manifestly alive state of being. This kind of waking up is realized through *zazen,* a form of meditation in which one learns to let go of thoughts and feelings and simply be present in the moment, with one's whole body and mind.

For centuries, Zen monasteries—places where monks reside permanently and others stay for short-term retreats—have devoted themselves to facilitating zazen. This practice lies at the heart of a monastery's existence, informing every minute of its schedule, every detail of its training, every aspect of its organization, every part of its facility, and every life within its walls.

Now that Zen has come to the West, the monastic tradition has been supplemented by lay institutions, including various custom-made kinds of Zen centers and *zendo*s (meditation halls). All of these places provide a space to practice zazen, and many also offer Zen-related training, workshops, talks, projects, and residencies.

In fact, Zen centers and zendos currently outnumber Zen monasteries in the West by a wide margin. The monastic way of life is just too uncommon here, at least for the time being, and too much at odds with the prevailing cultural trends of secularism, consumerism, and the pursuit of independent lifestyles.

Nevertheless, Zen monasteries, sanctioned as they are by the committed lives of the monastic residents, remain perhaps the best environments in the West for engaging in pure practice and for exploring the full range of teachings and experiences that are associated with Zen. Given the steady, rapidly expanding growth of interest in Zen among Americans in the past few decades, it seems inevitable that more and more monasteries will be founded here in the years to come.

This book uses Zen Mountain Monastery in Mt. Tremper, New York, as a model for depicting what it's like to spend time inside one of them. Many of the most basic, Zen-related experiences that are obtainable there can also be encountered during a visit to any other Zen monastery, center, or zendo. Some minor to major differences may exist from place to place, according to the particular tradition, teacher, community, or resources involved.

I've had the good fortune to be a student at Zen Mountain Monastery since 1994. I'm not a Zen teacher, and Zen is not something that's easy to teach anyway, even for those most qualified to do so— men and women who have practiced and studied intensively for a long period of time and who, as an acknowledgement of their understanding, have received formal transmission from a recognized master. However, I am familiar with Zen Mountain Monastery, with many of the people who live and visit there, and with a variety of other Zen communities in North America, and I welcome this opportunity to be a guide in your Zen travels.

To convey a more candid and visceral sense of what Zen practice can be like, and to ensure that certain statements are taken solely as my own impressions, I frequently speak in the first person in these pages. I also quote numerous other individuals—deliberately chosen to represent a broad spectrum of personalities and backgrounds—so that you can hear other voices and points of view besides mine.

At the end of the book is a list of recommendations for further reading and an extensive glossary containing the Zen and Buddhist words and phrases that appear in this text as well as many others. I encourage you to browse through the glossary as a means of familiarizing yourself with some of the terms, concepts, and conventions that prevail in a Zen environment. In the book as a whole, each new Zen or Buddhist word or phrase is briefly defined when it is first introduced, the glossary providing an additional or alternative source of information. A separate appendix features a list of selected places in the United States and Canada offering Zen-related services, programs, or retreats that are open to the public.

For the benefit of readers unfamiliar with Zen, I feel obliged to give a few notes about language issues in the text. All non-English words are either Japanese, the native language of Zen, or Sanskrit, the native language of Mahayana Buddhism, of which Zen is one school. To clarify any uncertainty, consult the glossary.

The Sanskrit word *buddha* (awakened one) is used in two contexts. The phrase "the Buddha" (with capitalization) is a title referring to the historical founder of Buddhism, named Siddhartha Gautama and also referred to as "Shakyamuni" (in Sanskrit, "sage of the Shakya clan"). The word *buddha* in lowercase refers to any awakened being: In Zen, everyone is believed to have buddha nature and to be capable of living the life of a buddha.

When I use the word *practice,* as in "spiritual practice," I mean the actual—not the trial—application of Zen principles and behaviors in one's ongoing life (an analogous usage in the professional world is law practice). Finally, in keeping with the policy at Zen Mountain Monastery, I use the word *monk* or *monastic* to refer to any person who has taken monastic vows, male or female.

The truth of Zen emerges only through personal experience. The same can be said about the truth of spending time in a Zen monastery, center, or zendo. It is my sincere hope that this book will prompt you to do just that, and will help make your stay all the more illuminating and enriching.

1

Coming Home to a Zen Place

Monk: "Where can I enter Zen?"
Master Gensha: "Can you hear the babbling brook?"
Monk: "Yes, I can hear it."
Master Gensha: "Then enter there."

Driving west on Route 28 in the Catskill Mountain region of New York, I felt my anxiety grow with every passing mile. I'd never been to Zen Mountain Monastery before. Now, in one of my earliest forays onto American Zen turf, I was spending a long weekend there. What would my stay be like? Each of the three words—*Zen, Mountain, Monastery*—sounded a dark, intimidating BONG! in my imagination. Would the weekend prove too alien, too difficult, too overwhelming? Perhaps even worse, would it be too boring?

The landscape rushing by my windows only reinforced my tension. Living just an hour's drive away, I'd witnessed its spectacular beauty in every season—its spring dance of wildflowers and a million budding shades of green; its lush summer foliage rolling luxuriously under a golden sky; its harlequin cloak of jewel-toned leaves in the fall; its winter mantle of crystalline snow setting off the stark splendor of black and evergreen branches. But today belonged to the gray, ragged end of February, and all I could see on either snowless, leafless, lifeless side of the road looked grimly inhospitable.

Then I turned off Route 28 onto Route 212 and, two miles later, drove through the front gate of Zen Mountain Monastery. I immediately felt a strange quiver deep in my gut, the exact center point of my body that I would later appreciate as my *hara,* a constant source of intuition and energy in Zen practice. "What *is* this odd sensation?" I wondered. Whatever it might be, it was quickly melting my anxiety. Then it dawned on me—I felt as if I were coming home.

I subsequently found out that embracing Zen Buddhism is often called coming home. In religious terms, the phrase refers to realizing our true buddha nature, the inherent perfection buried deep within us beneath layers of conditioning.

But how do we translate this kind of "coming home" into everyday language? What does it mean for each of us individually, regardless of how much we know, or don't know, about Zen Buddhism?

On a personal level, "coming home" evokes images of returning to childhood, a period when we experienced a fuller, more authentic sense of physical, mental, and emotional aliveness. Socially, it implies rediscovering our place in the world and our kinship with others in the human community. From a universal perspective, it suggests discarding our prickly egos altogether, even releasing our mad grip on the hominid agenda, and merging with the natural world.

Zen monasteries strive to foster all these dimensions of coming home in three basic, traditional ways. First, they provide a sacred space: a physical home environment for living in a spiritual manner. Second, they connect the individual to a vigorous *sangha* (Buddhist community) and to a specific human heritage of teachings that have been passed down through the ages from one person's mind to another's. Third, they serve as a secure base from which any practitioner can find and explore various paths to spiritual enlightenment.

Let's start by focusing on the sacred space. Physically the entrance and main building of a monastery are traditionally designed to greet people in a quietly impressive, spiritually inviting way and to mark off gently but clearly a safe haven from the outside world. Inside the main building, the most important physical space is a zendo (meditation hall). Usually it's a large room furnished with little but rows of *zafus* (round sitting cushions) mounted on *zabutons* (padded mats roughly thirty inches square) and an altar at one end. The layout is formal, giving every person his or her own well-defined territory and encouraging orderly, peaceful coexistence.

Other typical rooms, each with its own sacred and practical design elements, include a buddha hall (for training sessions and special ceremonies), a kitchen, a dining hall, and various administrative and living quarters. If the monastery sits on enough land, there could also be a Zen garden (specially designed to inspire meditation), a tea house, and even a cemetery—all reinforcing the notion of a monastery as a self-contained community.

The sacred space as a whole, indoors and out, tends to reflect the Zen aesthetic, which, among other elements, involves a reverence for simplicity and natural beauty. Within this space, people literally reteach themselves how to sit, breathe, eat, walk, see, and think in the most mindful, spiritually nourishing manner. It's very much like becoming a child all over again, with a second chance at evolving to realize one's true, perfect self. Because of the many communal activities on the day-to-day schedule, people also learn how to interact with each other more cooperatively, compassionately, and genuinely.

This latter point directs us to the second way in which Zen monasteries help a person come home: by connecting him or her more significantly with other individuals and with humanity in general. Besides nurturing a strong, highly interactive sangha that vows daily to save all sentient beings, each monastery conscientiously keeps alive a particular lineage of teaching, one that can be traced person to person from the abbot and other resident teachers all the way back almost twenty-five hundred years to the Buddha himself. The result is an especially vital human link between the life of every person attending the monastery and Buddhist lives throughout history. Each monastery also tells and retells its own well-polished stories about the people who created it, shaped its development, or somehow left their indelible imprint.

The third dimension of coming home—having a steady, reassuring base from which to explore various paths to enlightenment—relates symbolically to a monastery's age-old function as a refuge for weary travelers. Anyone who enters its front door is welcome, regardless of his or her background, beliefs, or objectives. Although being there requires following the monastic schedule, it doesn't represent setting foot on the road toward becoming a monk or even a Buddhist. Instead, you are left to choose or not to choose among the opportunities available. Monasteries usually offer different kinds of programs to pursue at your own pace depending on whether your interest in Zen is philosophical, artistic, or religious, and if the latter, whether you want to develop a lay practice or become a monastic. Often different residency options are also available: from a week or a month to a season or a year.

Entering Space and Time

Let's return to the Zen Mountain Monastery entrance and that raw February afternoon when I first drove through the front gate. What did I see that helped me feel I was coming home?

First of all, I perceived that the monastery *was* a home. A sign at the gate stated the days and hours when it was closed to the public, and here and there the grounds bore visible clues of domestic, hands-on care: for example, small, weathered birdfeeders stuffed with fresh seed;

long, straight branches stuck into either side of the gravel driveway to mark its boundaries in the event of a heavy snowfall; and a woman wearing patched jeans and several layers of jackets sweeping a stone walkway.

Not being familiar with monasteries, I had somehow assumed they were more or less public buildings, open daily to all, like most large Christian churches, Jewish temples, and holistic spiritual centers. This place was palpably one where people not only lived but where they cherished living and, therefore, where they did what they reasonably could to protect their privacy.

The main building itself fills your view from the gate, not to mention your imagination. It's a massive, handsome structure with meticulously laid stone walls and a steeply pitched, timber-framed roof soaring upward into open sky. It possesses a venerable style all its own that is simultaneously reminiscent of a Reformation-era church, a well-built colonial fortress, and a great Adirondack lodge, with elements of Quaker and, yes, Japanese form-fits-function spareness.

Actually, the main building is a rare example of Scandinavian Arts and Crafts architecture, built in 1930 as a spacious, stately retreat house for young Roman Catholic men. The monastery bought it in 1980, and in 1994 helped in having it declared a state and federal historic landmark.

Perhaps because I'm a professional storyteller, the main building profoundly appealed to the child in me right from the start. In my eyes, it didn't reflect any particular epoch. Instead, it seemed to be a once-upon-a-time place, like a folktale temple where characters from "Snow White," "The King of the Golden River," and other such tales might go to services.

Adding to this impression were the hand-wrought, heavily oxidized metal hinges adorning the front door. Among the sculptural elements they sported were a trio of lifelike birds (one of them looking directly at me), a squirrel, and a snail. The handle I pushed to go inside was, appropriately, an arrow arching to point the way.

On succeeding days, I noticed similar creatures or images worked into other doorway or casement parts, as well as carved into small nooks in various wood and stone structural elements. Early on, they helped give me a sense that I could find my own little niche there as well.

It's often said that Americans have historically been haunted by the specter of homelessness. First they struggled to settle a strange land. Since then, they've had to cope with the increasing fragmentation of family life and the trend toward changing one's residence and lifestyle more and more frequently during the course of a lifetime. As a result, they tend to be perpetually hungry for something they can truly recognize as home. This craving is achingly apparent in one of the nation's greatest home-bred myths, *The Wizard of Oz*, where the entire quest is basically to get back home.

To me, there is something Oz-like about Zen Mountain Monastery's main building that is wondrously in keeping not only with the setting itself—a cinemagenic mountainscape full of the same kinds of stone and wood as are in the building itself—but also with the whole grand venture of American Buddhism, an amalgam of the exotic and the familiar, of age-old mystery and contemporary yearning.

I still can't help perversely glimpsing an Oz-like quality from time to time when I practice there. Come to think of it, I undergo similar moments at other North American Zen communities as well. It can happen, for example, while I'm doing *kinhin* (walking meditation), a standard Zen practice to encourage greater mindfulness while engaging in a simple physical activity. For an instant, as I weave around and around rows of cushions with numerous other folks in rhythmic, silent, single file, our eyes downcast and our hands clasped at the waist, it can seem as if I'm following the yellow brick road, trusting it will eventually lead me to an all-knowing wizard. In reality, proper kinhin is a far different matter!

After entering the main building that February afternoon, I report-

Here we see the main building of Zen Mountain Monastery, the south side. The entrance is left of center, in the taller half of the building. The other half houses the zendo above the dining hall. The sloping masonry conceals steps leading up to a zendo door.

ed to the office and picked up a daily schedule. The first event I spotted took me aback, not the least because of its specificity: "Be seated in the zendo by 4:20 A.M." Next I parked my bags underneath a lower bunk in one of the spartan dormitory rooms and went on a quick tour led by a resident.

Wandering through the four-story interior, I confronted dim lighting, thick walls (some of them stone), and narrow, labyrinthine passageways opening onto large, ceremonial spaces. These features made the building seem alternately like a medieval cathedral, castle, or prison. Over the years to come, each of these images would occasionally revisit my imagination at times that were symbolically appropriate to the current state of my practice.

For the moment, I couldn't settle on any one perspective. My monkey mind, the cavorting, garrulous beast inside my head that I was hoping Zen might tame, was too busy processing data, desperately trying to figure out my position here. At the threshold of the zendo—the building's largest room, occupying most of the second and third floors—the monkey did stop to smile with a certain measure of relief. There, on a neat little plaque hung on a wall-mounted seating chart was my name: JACK. Inside the zendo, a third of the way up one of the long aisles of zabutons, I finally found my designated home here, a thirty-inch-square black zabuton with a wooden plaque beside it also saying JACK, a sight dear and consoling to the monkey's heart.

Every zendo I've visited, including this one, has had the same power to call me to spiritual attention. The overwhelming impact is a paradoxical blend of *emptiness*—caused by the absence of furniture or any other barrier to seeing or being seen—and *form*, apparent in the rigorously straight rows of evenly spaced zabutons arranged around the altar, upon which every element is placed according to a liturgically dictated geometry.

A core theme in Buddhism is the indivisible correspondence of emptiness and form. It's best reflected in the *Heart Sutra*, the most commonly recited sutra (scripture) in Zen communities: "Form is exactly emptiness, emptiness exactly form." (The *Heart Sutra* can be found in appendix C.) A traditionally well-organized zendo serves as a physical expression of this teaching.

At that first sight of Zen Mountain Monastery's zendo, a finely proportioned room with deep-set, multipaned windows and a high, vaulted ceiling, I was reminded of another kind of space that can stir up analogous feelings of awe and reverence: a cemetery. With its well-ordered plots, each dedicated to a particular human being, a cemetery shows us that all individuals rank equally in death. In a zendo, however, the zabutons evoke images of living people, who sit precisely to break through the half sleep of everyday existence and become even more alive.

Looking around a zendo, you get the message that all individuals are equal in life *and* death. The whole atmosphere is one of simplicity, solemnity, and infinite possibility—again, much like childhood in the purest sense of the word.

As I roamed through the rest of the building on my own, including the large, baronial dining hall immediately beneath the zendo and the big, busy (if vocally silent) kitchen, I was struck repeatedly by the combination of grand design and homespun detail. For all its timeless stone-and-wood monumentality, the building is palpably a work in progress.

Outside I'd noticed various minor repairs going on: for example, a scaffold across one wall and a drainage trench half dug along one of the walkways. Inside, I saw no such signs of current repair work, but I did observe many humble but skillfully wrought past improvements that helped give the space its own personal and interpersonal character: cabinets for liturgical and domestic supplies built precisely into alcoves; a Buddhist bookstore and two robe-changing rooms tucked neatly into opposing corners of the dining hall, like interlocking pieces in a Chinese box; a large bell and a *han* (striking board for summoning people) fitted perfectly into the zendo's vestibule wall at the junction of two staircases, so that their sound could be heard all over the building.

It's the type of phenomenon one frequently beholds in other American Zen monasteries, centers, and zendos—the gradual, lovingly engineered transformation of sites originally built for other purposes into functioning Zen spaces. Indeed, staying in one of these places typically involves helping in some way to build it: a reminder that the West is still a new frontier for Zen, and that making a home for it here often requires an extra amount of strictly physical labor.

I still had an hour before the first scheduled event that day, so I took a walk around the grounds. The monastery sits on 235 forested acres at the base of the southern bowl of Mt. Tremper. Its opposite boundaries are marked by two big streams—the Beaverkill and the Esopus—that converge a short distance below the front gate. According to both Feng-shui, the ancient Chinese art of geomancy, and local Native American (Lenape tribe) lore, this kind of natural configuration is especially auspicious and powerful.

It's easy to believe such a judgment as you climb a well-kept dirt road leading up Mt. Tremper from the monastery's parking lot. Immediately you're engulfed in a natural world thriving with a special vigor, obvious to me even on that scrappy day in February: the combined result of the land's own singular charms and the monastery's sensitive stewardship. Above your head soar gracefully swaying Eastern white pines. To your left murmurs a brook cascading over rocks speckled with emerald-green moss you can sometimes smell in the air. And all about you roam other animals—large, small, and in between. Among them may be a deer so tamed by life on monastery land that you almost bump into it. It could be foraging for food, or perhaps it's merely strolling with the same sense of being at one with the place that you, too, quickly develop.

I soon came to a tall *torii*, or trellislike open gateway, on the right side of the path, framing a Zen garden just beyond it. Zen gardens feature simple rock and plant components artfully arranged to suggest miniature landscapes. They can be found at many American monasteries, centers, and zendos and are sometimes even cultivated by Zen practitioners at home. Not only do they inspire a reflective, meditative calm that's conducive to zazen but also they testify to the creative harmony that can exist between human beings and the rest of nature—an important Zen teaching.

This garden, designed by Stephen Morrell, a landscape architect and a student at the monastery, uses basic Zen garden elements to represent mountains and rivers. It's a tribute to the monastery's own Mountains and Rivers Order, a name chosen to reflect both the place itself—as traditional in Zen—and the *Mountains and Rivers* text composed by Dogen, a highly revered twelfth-century Zen master.

The garden's focal point is a group of three large stones representing the three directional forces in nature: vertical (heaven), horizontal (earth), and diagonal (the bridge between). In front of this grouping flows a "river" of small, smooth, water-sculpted rocks that forks into two branches on the left. The landscape around these rivers is fashioned from locally gathered moss, fern, sedge, and low-bush blueberries.

Looking around me that day, I quickly discerned that I'd stumbled into a much more diversified sacred space than I'd first thought. Behind the bench where I sat admiring the garden stood a large pinewood, three-walled stage topped with a peaked roof. I later learned it was built to be the altar section of an outdoor Christian chapel prior to the monastery's tenure. Among the cut-out designs on its front half-walls you can still see communion chalices.

In the years since, however, this structure has become a recognizably Buddhist one. Today it's presided over by a large hand-carved, one-ton stone replica of the Buddha of Sarnath, widely considered one of the most beautiful statues of the Buddha ever created (Sarnath is the town in India where the Buddha first taught). Donated to the monastery in 1999 by Stewart Perrin, an art dealer, it now looks very much at home sitting in its high-peaked open window. Perrin exclaimed at the dedication ceremony, "It was as if this buddha fell to earth and landed here!"

But that was five years after my first walk, when the space was occupied by a much smaller buddha who also seemed to have chosen the place himself. Turning from this earlier buddha to look beyond the other side of the garden, I saw a clearing encircled by an especially magnificent stand of towering pines. Within it, a dozen wooden planks, about the shape and size of cricket mallets and covered with Japanese *kanji* (writing characters), were stuck endwise into the ground in random spots. The dates on these planks bore witness that this area was a cemetery, its small size testifying to the comparatively short time that both the monastery and American Zen have been in existence.

At the far end of the cemetery now stands a stupa (shrine) containing the ashes of Taizan Maezumi, Roshi—who was both the monastery's first abbot and the current abbot's teacher—who died in 1996. A striking, eight-foot stone monument with a square base supporting a stair-stepped pyramid, the stupa is an original, American-style variation of the more traditional dome-capped or pagoda-shaped Asian stupa.

After walking through the cemetery that first time, I returned to the path and continued climbing, the brook still babbling by my side. Within minutes I reached a bridge crossing the brook in front of Basho Pond. Here was—and is—yet another kind of sacred space encouraging a meditative frame of mind. The pond is named for the renowned seventeenth-century Japanese Zen poet, Basho, perhaps best known for this deceptively simple, essence-capturing verse:

> *The old pond;*
> *A frog jumps in—*
> *The water's sound.*

On the other side of the bridge, I took the downward path heading back toward the monastery. Along the way I passed quaint wooden cabins whose covered porches were crammed with branches and logs for burning. All in all, they were picture-perfect replicas of homesteads from the pioneering days, except, perhaps, for the occasional clay image of the Buddha peeking out of the kindling. Soon afterward I discovered that these cabins serve as lodgings for a number of the monks and temporary residents, who stock their own wood stoves in cold weather and share a common bathhouse. Two years later, I briefly lived in one of these cabins.

I came out of the forest some distance above the monastery and was stopped by a view I have since returned to enjoy many times. On the right is a big sweep of meadow running the rest of the way downhill.

In good weather, kinhin (walking meditation) is often conducted outdoors rather than inside the zendo.

The base of the meadow extends several hundred feet from the main building on the bottom left to a smaller, white-frame building (Dharma Communications, the monastery's publishing company) and a vegetable garden on the bottom right. Beyond the base of the meadow, the forest resumes, rising to a range of mountains farther west. Regularly mowed, often by the abbot himself, bobbing along on his beloved red tractor, the meadow functions as a vast, open plain for tranquilizing the mind and invigorating the body.

But it's the entire space—the meadow and everything around it—that communicates such a profound sense of home to countless visitors and residents. At the end of a flagstone path arcing down from the top of the meadow, the main building sits nestled in the center of this gently rounded basin of land, pulling you toward it from all directions.

I've caught sight of the building from the top of the path at many different hours of the day and night during each season of the year. My favorite time, however, is first thing in the morning—around 4 A.M.—in the winter, when the stars still shine brilliantly in the deep, dark sky, a meadowful of snow sparkles back below, and warm, flame-colored light glows out of the building's stone-framed windows. It is then that the monastery seems like a great, beating heart helping to keep the whole world alive.

Encountering the Three Treasures

The three treasures of Buddhism are the Buddha, the dharma, and the sangha. Each of these treasures can be understood in both a specific and a general way. *The Buddha* can refer both to the historical Buddha, the enlightened teacher of the late sixth and early fifth century BCE, and to the buddha nature that exists within each sentient (or living) being. *The dharma* can refer both to the official body of Buddhist teachings and to the entire phenomenal universe, every part of which provides its own teachings. *The sangha* can refer both to the group of people forming a particular Buddhist community (in American Zen: a monastery, center, or zendo) and to all sentient beings, who are inextricably interdependent.

The three treasures are woven into all aspects of a Zen community's existence, but they are perhaps most evident in the student-teacher relationship, the core of Zen training. As I said before, an authentic teacher, one who has received transmission in a particular lineage, can trace his or her authority from mind to mind back to the Buddha himself, thus serving as a true, living connector of Buddha, dharma, and sangha.

On the wall next to my home altar hangs a chart naming the seventy-nine other people who link my teacher, Abbot John Daido Loori of Zen Mountain Monastery, to the Buddha. During Sunday service at the monastery, the sangha chants all of these names. Inclusion in such a lineage verifies that the teacher has demonstrated to his or her teacher in every aspect of his or her being a clear, enlightened understanding of the dharma. It's a far cry from simply passing an exam, having a peak experience, or hearing the call.

Many Zen communities are not led by people who have qualified themselves in this way, although they may still call themselves teachers. Before you become involved in any sangha, it's a good idea to check into the leader's background to ensure that he or she has received genuine training in the dharma according to a specific lineage, or that he or she has received transmission and actually belongs to that lineage. Chapter 3 examines this issue in more detail.

Daido Roshi (Daido being his dharma name, meaning "great way"; Roshi being a title meaning "venerable teacher") is among the very few Zen teachers in the world who are recognized holders of both Soto and Rinzai lineages of Japanese Zen. The Soto school is associated with *shikantaza* ("pure sitting") zazen, while the Rinzai school includes both zazen and the study of koans (truths that can be grasped only by the buddha mind, not the logical one). He received transmission from Taizan Maezumi, Roshi, one of the foremost Japanese fathers of American Buddhism and founder of the Zen Center of Los Angeles, where Daido trained.

However, like any Zen master, Daido remains, first and foremost, an ordinary human being. When I first laid eyes on him, I didn't yet know who he was. He had just come off the aforementioned tractor and was passing through the dining hall where I sat waiting for dinner to start. His air of self-confidence and command clearly showed he was a leader, but of what? A tall, stocky, sixty-something Italian guy in fatigues, with a shaved head and a large, unreadably old tattoo on his forearm, he looked like the top honcho of a survivalist group or the foreman of a decidedly heavy construction crew.

Soon Daido's easy smile and instant rapport with everyone he met dispelled any intimidating aura I may have visualized earlier. That evening I watched him enter ceremoniously into the zendo wearing his formal robes, and I was impressed with his bearing in an altogether different way than I'd experienced before. Here was a man who radiated strength, integrity, grace, and a total engagement in what he was doing.

Subsequent weeks, months, and years revealed additional characteristics, most of which I've observed in other Zen teachers as well. They tend to possess a fundamentally deep, reassuring patience, despite the enormous amount of repetition and potential for frustration in their work. When necessary, they also display a bracing, no-nonsense directness in pointing out sloppy thinking or behavior. They don't invite personal attachments. Instead, they cultivate a selfless compassion that resists doing for students what the students need to do for themselves and that deflects inappropriate feelings of gratitude, dependence, or hero worship.

As far as I can tell, judging from my own interactions with about ten different representatives of the species, as well as from the comments of others, Zen teachers also share an ability to present a bare, expressionless, but fully attentive face to students during one-to-one teaching encounters. The effect is sometimes unnerving, sometimes emboldening, but it always challenges the student to dig to the deepest truth of the matter at hand.

Of course, each teacher also has a distinct personality based on his or her own particular life experience. Daido's background is remarkable in the extent to which it reflects the steady growth of American interest in Zen since the end of World War II and many of the reasons for that growth.

Born a first-generation Italian American in the middle of the Great Depression, Loori (later Daido) was raised in a very poor, Roman Catholic area of Jersey City, New Jersey, where he learned to survive on the streets by his wits and his fists. Fortunately, he also received a good dose of culture and an introduction to photography—a lifelong passion—at a boys' club sponsored by a wealthy local benefactor. Thus, like many Americans who were ultimately attracted to Buddhism in the decades to come, he grew up as a walker between worlds: in his case, European and American, sacred and profane, street smart and civilized, impoverished and enriched.

While still a teenager, Loori joined the navy and spent the Korean War on or near the front line, an experience that not only taught him the value of discipline and gave him his tattoo but also introduced him—as it did many other Americans—to Zen Buddhism. He went on to marry, start a family, and become a high-ranking research scientist in food chemistry. He was leading a life of wealth, corporate power, worldly success, and more and more palpably, spiritual deprivation. Again we see a common phenomenon in recent decades: That same pattern of high achievement but low satisfaction has spurred many Americans on a journey toward Zen.

Loori's love of photography eventually carried him to the very threshold of Zen. Already proficient in the art, he decided to turn it into a full-time career during the late 1960s. During this period he became a student of Minor White, who, besides being a famous American photographer, was a Zen practitioner.

Inspired by White's example, Loori started meditating daily. Soon he was regularly attending events at the Zen Center of Los Angeles (ZCLA). What had originally been an artistic and philosophical impulse in his life was thereby transformed into a spiritual direction—a means of coming to Zen for many Americans during the turbulent 1960s, the "me decade" 1970s, and afterward.

As the 1970s progressed, so did Loori's commitment to Zen. Now bearing his dharma name Daido, he took monastic vows at ZCLA. In 1980 he traveled to the New York City area on behalf of ZCLA to help start a community there, and within a few months he found himself standing for the first time on the Mt. Tremper property, admiring the main building. Much to my delight, I found out recently that his first thought was, "It's just as if I were coming home."

I can only speculate what "coming home" might have meant to Daido then. On the most obvious level, he was back in the area of the United States where he'd grown up. He had also previously developed an affection for this very part of New York, having led several photography workshops in nearby Woodstock. In fact, for most of his life he'd sought refuge in the wilderness and had regularly gone on hunting treks in similar terrain farther north: originally with a rifle and later, as his consciousness evolved, with a camera.

That day when Daido first came to Mt. Tremper, he was shopping for a building he could use as the nucleus of a Zen arts center. He'd expected to settle for some small, wood-framed, sale-priced chapel. Now he was drinking in the sight of a grand, almost cathedral-like edifice, about the same age as he was, that, like him, had started out Catholic and had passed through several metamorphoses since.

Most recently, the building and site had been a Lutheran camp under the devoted, energetic leadership of Harold and Ruth Haar. After Daido heard the Haars' bottom asking price—$240,000—he said to himself, "This is insane! I have no money! I make $100 a month as a monk!"

Abbot John Daido Loori, Roshi, is the spiritual leader of Zen Mountain Monastery and one of its three resident teachers.

But the spiritual resonance Daido felt for the place kept growing stronger, and so did his confidence that others would appear to help support his dream. Meanwhile, the Haars, having already been approached by commercial developers, were thrilled at the prospect of turning over their property to someone who seemed to care about it as much as they did and who was planning to use it for religious purposes.

In no time, Daido and Harold Haar were standing in the meadow next to the main building shaking hands on the deal. As they did, a shadow passed across them. Looking up, Daido saw a great blue heron flying overhead—a majestic bird he had long quested, fruitlessly, to photograph. "In the words of Carlos Castaneda's teacher Don Juan," he later commented, "it was an affirmation of nature."

The very day Daido and his two sons moved onto the property, he started sitting zazen. One by one, others came to join him. The place barely survived that first winter. With no heat in the zendo, Daido's new students had to sit wearing layers of coats, gloves, and hats. He could gauge the quality of their zazen by the steadiness of their breath, clearly visible in the air. One morning was so cold that the ceramic vase on the altar split and fell apart, but the flowers still stood tall in a cylinder of solid ice.

Much to Daido's wonder, large checks from well-to-do lenders appeared at the last minute to keep the bank from foreclosing on the mortgage. Nevertheless, Daido doesn't credit money for making the Zen Arts Center and, subsequently, Zen Mountain Monastery, survive. "It came to be," he says, "because of the vitality of zazen."

Zen Mountain Monastery and the Mountains and Rivers Order have since grown steadily larger and, in the process, more influential throughout the American Zen world. In 1987 Daido received transmission from Maezumi Roshi, which allowed him to assume formal abbotship of Zen Mountain Monastery, a post previously held in absentia by Maezumi Roshi. To ensure that Zen Mountain Monastery received full recognition as an authentic Zen training environment, Daido traveled to Japan to have his new status officially confirmed by the parent Soto school in an elaborate, traditional ceremony.

At present, Daido has about three hundred formal students of his own and teaches to countless thousands of other people who come to the monastery from all over the world for services, talks, retreats, or residencies. Maezumi Roshi and Harold Haar, both mentors of the monastery's past, are buried in the monastery's cemetery; and Daido's two recently transmitted dharma heirs, Bonnie Myotai Treace, Sensei, and Geoffrey Shugen Arnold, Sensei (*sensei* meaning "teacher"), are actively helping to ensure the monastery's future survival and growth.

Daido's story is worth knowing if only because he is a significant figure in the history of American Zen. Trained by Maezumi Roshi during the 1970s, when Zen had yet to achieve mainstream popularity, he became one of the first American-born teachers of Zen. Now he's among the most prominent, with numerous publications, tapes, workshops, and public appearances to his credit. In Zen Mountain Monastery and the Mountains and Rivers Order, he has created an extensive, uniquely dynamic network of Zen Buddhist temples, practice centers, and sitting groups throughout the United States and abroad.

Daido's story is also noteworthy because it illustrates so much of the cultural history, and so many of the personal issues, that have led Americans to turn toward Zen. Despite the dharma's exotic appearance as an Asian import, the reality from a Zen perspective is that the dharma is universal, and its increasing manifestation among Americans can be regarded as a natural, inevitable development in the evolution of the country and its people.

There is, however, another important purpose in reviewing Daido's story—or the story of *any* Zen teacher one is seriously considering—and that is to shed more light on the human life behind the teaching. According to Zen, we must come to realize enlightenment out of our own experience, not out of any kind of separation from that experience. Zen practice demands that we become more and more aware of who we are, how we have been conditioned, what our predispositions and motivations are, and what lessons and powers our personal history has to offer.

A primary reason why Daido and most other American-born Zen teachers are so effective in their work is that they themselves have been integrally involved in the real world of American life and know first-hand the stresses, strains, temptations, and opportunities that their students confront. They've also arrived at Zen practice in many of the same ways that their students have, and they can testify all the more credibly to the real value of what they're teaching.

Walking the Way

The first time you attend any sort of official gathering in a Zen monastery, center, or zendo—whether it's for a service, sitting, or talk—you may be struck right away by the distinctly different types of clothing you see. Some individuals may be dressed in robes. Among them may be people wearing cloth rectangles that hang biblike from their neck to cover their abdomen. Other individuals may wear one of these rectangles but no robe. For the most part, the rest of the group is likely to be garbed in simple, modest clothing, predominantly black.

This being the land of the free, you may also spot a few loud prints, safari shorts, pastel ski pants, tank tops, strapless halters, mohair sweaters, or high-impact accessories, depending on the season, the neighborhood, and the recent degree of mass-market attention to Buddhism. This category of very casual or trendy dress conveys its own significant messages about Zen in America, but I'll reserve them for later.

What about the robes, the rectangles, and the plain, mostly black clothes? What's the key to this multilevel, apparently Zen-based fashion code?

Let's begin with the robes. The meaning of robes can vary from place to place. In some, everyone wears the same color robe; in others, robes are not worn at all. However, a robe typically designates an official student of Zen Buddhism, someone who has entered into a formal teacher-student relationship with a Zen master and, in most communities, has simultaneously become a member of a particular Zen training order. The student may be a monk or a layperson. If a layperson, the student may or may not have taken formal Buddhist vows, that is, have embraced Buddhism as a religion.

Zen monks, male or female, generally dress in a black robe, with an additional outer robe of black (called a *kesa*) that's draped across one shoulder. Teachers—who are almost always monks—typically wear a

On their way to the zendo after an outdoor ceremony, students pass beside a stone dragon mounted on a low wall. In Zen an enlightened being is called a dragon; a deluded being, a snake. Dragons are also symbolic guardians of Zen places. White or gray robes indicate lay students in this monastery. Nonstudent residents for a month or more, considered provisional students, are also gray-robed. Black robes are worn by monastics.

gold kesa instead of a black one. They may also have other robes in various muted colors that they wear on different occasions, especially if they function as the abbot of a monastery or the leader of an order.

Students who are not monks may or may not wear a robe, depending on the custom of the place or order. If they do, their robe may also be black, but more often it's some other somber color like gray or brown. A white robe in the Japanese Zen tradition denotes a lay student in a relatively advanced stage of training, the home-dwelling counterpart of a monk.

At Zen Mountain Monastery, nonmonastic students have gray robes. This middle-tone hue is symbolic. Some of these students never go on to take Buddhist vows. Instead, they pursue Buddhism as a philosophical or ethical belief system. They may even practice another religion while continuing to wear the gray robe of a Buddhist student. Others eventually do take vows: a matter not just of personal choice but also of approval by the teacher and a so-called "guardian council" of senior students. The vow taking occurs during a traditional Zen ceremony called *Jukai* that's roughly akin to a Christian confirmation or a Jewish bar or bat mitzvah.

If these gray-robed students later enter the monastic path, they don a black robe. If, instead, they progress along a lay path, they may eventually reach a stage in their training where they begin wearing a white robe. Thus a person in gray who takes vows has the potential of proceeding in one direction to become a person in black or in another to become a person in white. When visiting a Zen monastery, center, or zendo for a weeklong retreat, you may or may not be asked to wear a robe.

Now, what is that biblike rectangle? It's a traditional Zen garment called a *rakasu* that is worn by a student who has taken religious vows. It represents a miniature version of the monk's kesa, having first been developed during a period in ancient China when Ch'an (or Zen) monks were subject to persecution and therefore concealed a smaller, robelike vestment beneath their everyday outer clothing. In more recent times the rakasu hangs proudly outside the robe or, when no robe is worn (due to local custom or for individual reasons), outside any other clothing.

At Zen Mountain Monastery, students follow tradition by sewing their own rakasus during a week in residence that culminates with their Jukai ceremony. It's a deceptively intricate garment, with a stylized, time-honored rice-paddy design of separate pieces that get sewn into the front panel; precisely-designed straps, one of which is broken over the heart and tied at either end to a small wooden circle; and a back panel that frames a piece of white silk on which the teacher inscribes (among other things) the student's new dharma name. The sewing process is also detailed. Specific kinds of stitches are prescribed for different parts of the rakasu, and as students sew each stitch, they chant to themselves, "one with the Buddha, one with the dharma, one with the sangha."

When you're coming into a Zen environment as a nonstudent, it's best to wear simple, modest, solid-colored clothing, preferably black or at least dark. In some cases you're explicitly advised to do so. In others you're left to learn on your own.

From a Zen perspective, this dress code serves a number of purposes. One is a very basic one: Dark clothes look tidy and don't show dirt or wrinkles as easily as lighter clothes do. Zen has always put a high value on practicality!

More important, this type of dress keeps you from being too self-preoccupied or too ego driven. Rather than drawing attention to yourself or expressing your individuality, you are doing what you can to render yourself unremarkable—not too fancy, not too ragged—so that you can become one with others. It also conveys respect for, and seriousness about, the occasion. Perhaps most significant of all, it doesn't distract others around you from focusing on the point of the gathering or from transcending their own egos to merge with the sangha that's present. In the universe, according to Zen, where all sentient beings are part of one reality, what you do for yourself is inseparable from what you do for others.

We have come back full circle to the category of people who wear loud prints, leather pants, tube tops, or other eye-catching gear. The fact that individuals with the best intentions wear such clothing to a Zen gathering without realizing their inappropriateness testifies not only to the novelty of Zen in America but also to the lack of experience many Americans have in attending religious assemblies of *any* kind.

Every religion aspires to bring people together both physically and spiritually. The clothing we wear in a religious setting can send a very clear signal of how much we sincerely share that aspiration or how far along we are toward realizing it. Zen in particular asks that we do as much as we can to actualize it.

Once you step inside a Zen monastery, center, or zendo—no matter who you may be—you assume a personal responsibility to *be* there in the most alive sense of the word. Even though you don't need to be a Buddhist to sit zazen in a Zen community or take part in the other practices there like bowing and chanting, the community and practices themselves are spiritual by nature. The assumption, therefore, is that you will enter into them in full spirit, as a gesture of oneness with the people around you, even if only for the moment. This type of "good faith" participation involves your whole mind and body—including, on literally the most superficial level, your clothing.

Regardless of clothing, path, or degree of training, anybody can usually take part in the basic activities that mark the calendar of a typical Zen monastery, center, or zendo, as well as engage in any special weekend or weeklong retreats and temporary residencies that the community offers. Sampling a variety of these activities enables you to determine through personal experience which particular route you want to follow in Zen: occasional explorer, ongoing participant, formal student, lay practitioner, or monastic.

In some cases, you may be interviewed over the phone, in person, or by correspondence before you're admitted to a particular event, program, or retreat. It's usually just to make sure that you know what's involved and can agree to the level of cooperation expected. Some of the typical interview issues are discussed in chapter 6.

Among the basic, regularly scheduled activities within most Zen communities are a weekly service including zazen (usually on Saturday or Sunday during the morning or early afternoon), various afternoon or evening holiday observances, and recurring periods of intensive practice called *sesshins*. Traditionally a sesshin involves sitting for most of the day in thirty- to forty-minute sessions broken up by kinhin, meals, caretaking, services, and rest periods. Silence is maintained throughout the sesshin (except when it's necessary for leaders to give directions), and usually other prohibitions are adopted to eliminate distractions, such as no reading, writing, or making eye contact.

Sesshins may last for a day, a weekend, a week, or ten days, depending on the institution or the specific occasion. They may occur as often as once a month in a given community or as rarely as once or twice a year. In many respects they provide the strongest, most revealing exposure to Zen practice that a Zen community can offer. However, because of their intensity, people with little or no comparable experience are usually advised to begin with short sesshins and gradually work up to longer ones.

In addition to regularly scheduled activities, many Zen monasteries, centers, or zendos also sponsor special retreats. Typically retreats feature common Zen practices—such as sitting zazen, perhaps for several, approximately thirty-minute sessions per day—combined with talks or activities organized around a specific Zen-related theme: for example, a particular master, sutra, precept, art form, or body practice; or the connection between Zen and a certain contemporary life issue, such as parenting, coping with serious illness, or entering the computer age.

Temporary residencies, lasting anywhere from a week or a month to one or more years, are a means of immersing oneself completely in the community's schedule. All temporary residents, regardless of background, are challenged to live in most respects like monks. Meanwhile, they get to take full advantage of everything the community has to offer.

In addition to these events, retreats, and residencies, a sizable Zen institution usually has its own formal training matrix: a systematic, stage-by-stage approach to studying and practicing Zen over the long term. Working within this matrix, each individual student belonging to the institution strives to acquire an increasingly deeper and broader understanding of Zen as it fits his or her own life. A visitor for a day, a weekend, a week, or even a month may or may not feel its impact, but most likely it is there, helping to shape his or her experience.

For this reason, as well as for learning more about Zen practice in general, you may want to investigate the various training matrices available in different places. Zen Mountain Monastery's "Eight Gates" program (briefly sketched in chapter 3) is one example.

Zen communities may also sponsor social action or outreach programs that are open to outside volunteers. Endeavors of this nature include helping the homeless or disabled, conserving the environment, providing disaster relief, assisting in health care, defending civil rights, contributing to public education, and a wide range of other compassionate projects.

In the following pages, I describe all of these types of activities and programs in more detail, focusing for example's sake on how they unfold at Zen Mountain Monastery. But before I do that, let's confront a more fundamental issue in the next chapter: Why get involved in them in the first place? After all, Zen can be a very difficult practice. Why bother? What draws people to Zen? What type of person might you encounter—or even become—once you enter a Zen environment?

2

Who Goes There?

Do not seek to follow in the footsteps of the men of old;
seek what they sought. —BASHO

Weather permitting, the most popular place to socialize at Zen Mountain Monastery lies just outside the heavy oak doors at the east end of the main building's dining hall. There, radiating from a semicircular plaza, a broad amphitheater of nine stone tiers rises up to ground level. They function as both stairs and sitting platforms.

During workshops or special occasions, people assemble at this outdoor forum to hear a talk or to pose for photographs. At more casual moments of the day, like after meals, they gather there in pairs or groups and chat about any topic from here to eternity. While they do, a striking conversation piece gazes down on them from the wall above the doorway: a fifteen-foot carved oak statue of Christ.

Created for the original Roman Catholic retreat house in 1938, the fully robed figure, dubbed "Bidding Christ" by its sculptor, William Hoppe, appears to have its arms raised in a welcoming or all-embracing gesture. The first-time observer may not notice for a while that the bluestone recess in which it stands is cross-shaped and that the entire sculpture-plus-setting is meant to symbolize the crucifixion, without depicting the agony usually associated with it.

The east wall of the main building houses an impressive fifteen-foot wooden statue, "Bodhisattva Christ." Below it are circular steps faced by a deeply recessed doorway. Students often gather in both places. The two-story window alcoves on either side of the doorway were designed to suggest altar candles: Note the stonework resembling rays of light.

Now called "Bodhisattva Christ" (a bodhisattva being an enlightened individual who postpones his or her final entrance into nirvana in order to save others), the statue seems a perfect image to unite the Christian and Buddhist legacies of the place. It also suggests similar kinds of integrations that are occurring on a broader scale. Although the figure in context is clearly Christ, the simplicity of the design and the naturalness of the material lend it such a Zen-like quality that you can easily read into it the coming of Buddhism to Judeo-Christian America. In fact, directly in back of the statue, on the other side of the stone wall, a wooden statue of the Buddha sits on the zendo altar that was once the church's main altar as well. Appropriately, the Buddha faces west.

The Bodhisattva Christ can also be taken to represent the dual-natured personal history of many of those who come here. A high percentage of them grew up as Christians but no longer feel connected with that religion. Maybe they can't reconcile their subsequent life experience or intellectual beliefs with the basic tenets of Christianity—at least as they understand them. Possibly they reject this faith because they suffered as children from overly rigid, scary, or unappealing expressions of it. Or perhaps they never bonded to it in any lasting way because of a childhood pattern of observance that was infrequent, mechanical, or lackadaisical. Yet, all of these people, to some degree, are left searching for the same promise of spiritual fulfillment that Christianity once held out to them.

Others still identify themselves as practicing Christians but want to revitalize, expand, or refine their faith by investigating what Buddhism has to offer. A few of them may even aspire to become Christian Buddhists (or Buddhist Christians, depending on their perspective). Many people see this hybrid identity as a viable option because Buddhism doesn't offer any conflicting or competing god of its own. As Daido often points out, Buddhism is not atheistic but, rather, *non*theistic: It just doesn't address the issue of whether or not there's a creator god. Thus Roman Catholic priests and nuns, for example, have come to Zen Mountain Monastery to study Buddhism as a means of enriching their Christian faith.

The absence of a creator god in Buddhism also makes it appealing to Jews—both those who retain their faith in God and those who don't. Referring to the highly visible number of so-called JuBus (Jewish Buddhists) in America, Rodger Kamenetz, author of *The Jew in the Lotus* (HarperSanFransicso, 1994) notes:

> In the past twenty years, JuBus have played a significant and disproportionate role in the development of [American Buddhism]. Various surveys show Jewish participation in such groups ranging from 6 to 30 percent. This is up to twelve times the Jewish proportion of the American population, which is 2½ percent. (p. 7)

Christian, Jew, or otherwise, if you live in America, you live in a culture that's profoundly Christian in character, and herein lies the most general appropriateness of the Bodhisattva Christ statue. America continues to think of itself as a grand national experiment in living on an ideal plane, synthesizing all the best that the world has to offer. And it's populated by individuals who tend to envision their own lives as the same type of personal experiment.

So what, specifically, brings some of these experimenters right up to the doorway of a Zen monastery?

In my own case, much to my chagrin, hindsight tells me it was a midlife crisis. At the time, I viewed it more narrowly as a health crisis. Shortly before my forty-eighth birthday, I sneezed and, as they say, threw out my back. Months of pain and despair ensued, as I hobbled my herniated disk to one expert after another, from osteopathic surgeons to massage therapists to crystal energy weavers. For several days in a row, I would manage to lead a more or less normal life of restricted movement, but inevitably there would come days when I was forced to lie motionless in bed.

Given my age, well beyond invincible youth, the situation was severe enough to raise a few of the main questions that Zen addresses: What is the meaning of life and death? How can I live more vibrantly? How can I face death with greater equanimity?

Eventually, the greatest peace I found was in practicing a kind of meditation and overall mindfulness I picked up, by example, from a friend. She practiced insight, or *vipassana,* meditation, a practice similar to zazen that comes from the Theravada Buddhist tradition of southeast Asia. I somehow felt it would be impertinent to ask her point-blank about her involvement in Buddhism. I must have thought deep down that it was something properly kept secret.

All by itself, this slight shift in my consciousness and behavior probably wouldn't have nudged me toward exploring Buddhism on my own if it hadn't been accompanied by a magic signal—which, incidentally, is the kind of statement I heard over and over again while interviewing people for this book. My signal occurred while I was seated alone in my friend's kitchen, waiting for her to return and trying my best to stonewall the escalating pain in my back. On the table in front of me lay a magazine I'd never seen before: *Tricycle: A Buddhist Review.* I flipped it open and immediately read these words:

> What kind of man is this, his shoulders bent, holding a stick to support him along the way? Even as I think of old age approaching, what pleasures now can these gardens afford, the years of my life like the fast-flying wind? ("Shakyamuni Buddha: A Life Retold," *Tricycle*, Vol. II, no. 4, p. 13)

It was Jack Kerouac's story of Prince Siddhartha encountering for the first time a sick, aging man: Siddhartha's initial step on the path to becoming the Buddha. I had long harbored separate intellectual interests in both Kerouac and Buddhism. Although I didn't mistake Kerouac as any kind of expert on Buddhism, I did identify with the kidlike yearning and struggling he had intermittently gone through during his adult years as he tried to live out his Buddhist inclinations. Suddenly, sitting in that kitchen, I felt as if Buddhist inclinations had just arisen in me—not by virtue of any romantic association with Kerouac and Siddhartha, despite its catalytic part in the magic, but as a result of my own, most authentic self responding directly, if inarticulately, to the questions I had just read.

I immediately began visiting different kinds of Buddhist communities. Finally, on that February day I described earlier, I came to Zen Mountain Monastery, knowing nothing about it except that it was near my house.

I have since realized that I was like many of the individuals in my age bracket who show up at the monastery: one of the most sizeable groups that do. Underneath the back pain, other, more metaphysical disturbances were setting the process in motion. My career as a writer and my sheer years of living, loving, and learning had already given me a sense of accomplishment, so what now? It was becoming more and more painfully obvious to me that I didn't have a whole lot of time left, so what about delving into those larger, harder-to-define concerns that I'd been putting off for so long, like seeing more clearly into the truth of things? What was I waiting for? How should I begin? Where could I find reasons for living beyond the pleasures of the garden?

Similar questions surface at different times in the lives of different individuals, but they especially pester people around age forty or older, as my interviews for this book confirmed. Other common motives for coming to a Zen community can also be ascribed to particular groups of human beings, but merely listing them by demographic category would be misleadingly simplistic. More to the point, dividing people into groups would be against the spirit of Buddhism. Instead, let's look at how reasons emerged in the life stories of several individuals who were generous enough to talk with me—people of diverse ages and back-grounds who one day found themselves sitting on the stone tiers out-side Zen Mountain Monastery's east doorway. Among these interviewees are first-time visitors, occasional retreatants, and residents: both short-term and long-term.

Sara: "a hopefully happy wanderer"

Besides people around forty years old, the other major group that comes to Zen Mountain Monastery (and, based on published reports, to Zen communities in general) are individuals in their early twenties. Sara speaks for many of her peers in this age range when she admits, "I'm still wondering who I am, what I'm capable of, why I'm here, what's the best thing I can do with my life." Much to the dismay of many of her family members and friends, these personal questions compelled Sara to drop out of college after two years. She has since been, as she puts it, "a hopefully happy wanderer."

Sara's odyssey began as an open-ended journey to find more personally engaging experiences than the ones she'd had as a college student. "I was getting good grades," she points out, "but I couldn't shake this feeling of falseness. I was doing it for the degree, for the education, for the jollies along the way. There was no real purpose to it. After my sophomore year, I felt totally numb about it. Why stay around? Why did I think I had to be there in order to grow as a person?"

Sara doesn't interpret her decision to leave college as a rejection of the academic way of life. In many respects, she still values that path very highly. Instead, what prompted her to go was the realization that the she wasn't really there in the first place. "I wanted to come alive again," she says. "I knew in my heart I could do much more for myself and for others if I got out into the world and figured out where I truly wanted to be. Maybe I'll wind up going back to college and picking up where I left off, but at least I'll really be there."

Knowing only what she'd read about Buddhism in her philosophy classes, Sara first heard about Zen Mountain Monastery while she was attending a yoga workshop at a holistic health center in Massachusetts. She was talking with one of the other retreatants there about her yearning for a lifestyle in which work and play, body and mind, spirituality and sociality all come together and nourish each other. He told her that the closest he'd come to that kind of life was a year he'd spent at Zen Mountain Monastery.

"The notion of a monastery threw me a bit," Sara confessed. "I'm Jewish and not what you'd call religious. But I'd just left a job where I'd made good money, and something about this guy really impressed me. So I called the monastery that afternoon and signed up for the next Zen training weekend.

Having now completed that weekend at the monastery, Sara is seriously considering spending a full month in residence as soon as she can arrange it. "This place turned out to be totally different from what I expected," she admits. "I imagined it would be more like [the holistic health center], with lots of time to rest, read, reflect, go your own way. It was far more intense than that. Some things got to me at first, always being told what to do, having to work as well as go to the classes. But when I gave myself to what was happening, I got so much back."

Sara now has a specific image to remind her of this experience: strawberries. "I was assigned to the garden crew for one of the caretaking sessions," she explains. "It was a wet, gray day outside and I'd been hoping to get something indoors and easy. But there I was, kneeling in the mud. To avoid feeling angry or sorry for myself, I devoted my full attention to weeding the strawberry patch exactly as I'd been told. It was amazing how connected I became with what I was doing, how alive I was, how alive the patch was. I'll never forget that."

Drew: *"voluntarily vulnerable"*

Drew falls somewhere between the twenties group and the forties group. By the calendar, he belongs to the latter; but his life history, which has repeatedly challenged him to redefine himself, gives him many spiritual points in common with the former.

For most of his adult life, Drew lived in various places abroad, first working for the Peace Corps in Africa and later teaching English as a second language in the Middle East, with occasional sojourns in Europe. In 1995 he returned to Albany, where he'd grown up, and began a new teaching career there. He was finally starting to settle down in life. As part of this process, he was even beginning to do Buddhist-style meditation at home—something that had intrigued him off and on for years but had not seriously become part of his life before.

Nevertheless Drew still felt adrift. "I wasn't sure who I was or wanted to be," he recalls. "Yes, I was back in my hometown, but I didn't quite know if I belonged there."

Drew began seeking a more personal sense of community at various nearby Buddhist places. On Easter Day 1996 that quest brought him to Zen Mountain Monastery for Sunday service. "I'm very self-conscious," he admits. "I didn't want to be late for my first visit, so I drove down and back on Good Friday to see how long the ride would take. I was determined to do everything exactly right."

Drew's self-consciousness persisted through his early experiences at the monastery. "I felt a little silly, like an outsider, that first Sunday," he remembers. "Most of those around me seemed as if they'd known each other for years, although that probably wasn't the case at all. This awkwardness of mine lasted for months. I didn't like exposing my ignorance about certain issues or activities that puzzled me, so I didn't ask the questions that would have made things much easier. I'm told I looked standoffish, when I was actually desperate to fit in."

Because Drew was mainly interested in meditating, he was also uncomfortable at first with the bowing and chanting that takes place in the service before zazen. "I was ambivalent about doing any kind of liturgy," he notes. "I'm an ex-Catholic, and that's one of the aspects of Catholicism I had a hard time accepting."

Despite these misgivings, Drew never missed a Sunday service at Zen Mountain Monastery for months afterward, and gradually he realized why. "I did sincerely feel drawn to the place," he says. "For a while I told myself I had to keep returning because the training might help me become the person I'd always wanted to be—nicer, more patient, more spiritual, et cetera, so I would like myself better. But then I felt it was where I already belonged, whatever flaws I might have."

Drew began a habit of coming earlier on Sundays so he could reconnect with the natural landscape of his new home before the service began. "One thing I like to keep track of is how Basho Pond changes as the seasons change," he says. "There's a statue of the Buddha on the far bank of the pond. At a certain time in the summer, it disappears in the high grasses that grow around it. Then it reappears in the fall."

Drew went on to became a student of the Mountains and Rivers Order and, twice since then, a month-long resident. "That first residency was an incredibly eye-opening experience," he reports. "I wanted everyone there to be my friend right away, almost as if I were a kid going to summer camp. Of course, it didn't work out that way, and I soon learned to be grateful for that. One of the best things about the month was that you didn't have to live up to other people's expectations. You could show up in a bad mood or screw up some way, and people would still accept you and share their lives with you in a very natural way."

This lesson and others have made Drew more and more appreciative of what the monastery does as well as what it doesn't do. "You bring yourself here with you," he emphasizes, "and you have to deal with that self on your own. The monastery doesn't promise comfort or coziness. Instead, it gives you a place where you can expand your horizons. To be open to that, you need to make yourself voluntarily vulnerable."

Robert: "the obvious next step"

As a systems engineer with his own company in Philadelphia, Robert was more self-confident, more financially secure, and more enthusiastic about his life than he'd ever been before. Then he and his longtime girlfriend began to talk about marriage.

"It may have been that decision to marry, to have a family, that started it all," Robert says. "I knew I wanted to take life more seriously, but I wasn't sure how. Just going through a ceremony wasn't going to make me a wise husband, a good father, or a more mature human being. I needed some guidance for that. I'd never really had any strong religious faith. When I found out about what was available at Zen Mountain Monastery, it seemed the obvious next step to check it out."

Robert first connected with the monastery via its website on the Internet. After a few exchanges with Cybermonk, the website's interactive contact (a rotating assignment among the monastics), he signed up for a weeklong workshop on Dogen's teachings. He hoped to acquire some sort of blueprint for personal growth through studying what one of the greatest Zen masters had to say.

"I approached the matter very scientifically," Robert declares. "I'd always considered Zen an intelligent religion. It engages the mind. In many ways it's compatible with relativity theory and even subatomic physics. I liked those things about Zen, and that's why I was turning to it, why I wanted to take the Dogen seminar. I was looking for a system of ethics and morality that made sense, that didn't have a lot of mysteries or mumbo jumbo I had to take sheerly on faith."

Instead, what Robert discovered—and briefly participated in—was a way of living that depended a great deal on faith. He'd just been through a week of learning to trust himself to realize what he couldn't yet understand, of becoming one with others around him whether he knew them well or not, and of putting himself into activities wholeheartedly without standing back to evaluate his moment-to-moment performance.

"The first-timers had to figure out how to do a lot of things just by following what the others were doing," Robert recalls. "I kept saying to myself, 'Why don't they give you a manual ahead of time explaining all this?' Then it hit me over the head that I was totally missing the point. It's an irony, really. Here I was, resenting stuff I had to take on faith, when Zen is, in fact, a religious faith. I didn't like that I had to find out so many things for myself, or learn by doing, and yet, that's what I was counting on Zen to help me with."

Some practices that Robert found mysterious that week were, in fact, explained in brochures that he had only quickly read through and forgotten. Others, however, were not, and Robert continued to wonder about them all through the week. Finally the truth dawned on him: What felt so strange to him was not really the practices themselves, or what they may or may not mean, but his own willingness to engage in them fully without needing to understand them intellectually. "It occurred to me that I liked the self-discipline you're encouraged to have at the monastery simply for its own sake," he says. "It gives structure and substance to the day. It kind of props you up and gives you energy."

Robert also realized that much of the guidance he was searching for was, in fact, within him. He reports, "This week I learned I was capable of doing all sorts of things I'd always wanted to do but didn't feel I was the type to do. I could get up before dawn. I could move from one activity to another without having to take a break. I could help to repair a wall even though I'm not a carpenter. I could wait in silence for minutes on end, standing perfectly still, and not feel bored but exhilarated."

Diane: "a wrong turn to the right place"

For Diane, a psychotherapist from Montreal, Zen Mountain Monastery came as a pleasant surprise during a weeklong visit to an old friend living in nearby Kingston, New York. "The story starts out pretty shameful," she says. "I wanted an excuse not to go to church with my friend and her mother on Sunday, so I told them I was planning to visit the monastery. I didn't even know it had a Sunday service, but I got here just as the service was starting. I was completely entranced by it, and the talk that day by the abbot seemed as if it were speaking directly to me." Reflecting on that morning now, she laughs, "You might say I took a wrong turn to the right place."

Soon after flying back to Montreal and resuming her heavy caseload of patients, Diane began feeling unmistakable symptoms of professional burnout. She decided to take a three-month sabbatical. "I was starting to wonder who I was apart from my job," she explains. "It was everything to me, and that was not a healthy attitude. Underneath lay a great deal of fear: What would happen to me if I failed at my job, or if I suddenly lost it? I knew the time had come to do some serious soul-searching of my own."

Remembering Zen Mountain Monastery as, in her words, "the last place I'd felt deeply moved," Diane dug out the monastery's catalog from her files and signed up for the next available retreat. "Coincidentally," she notes, "it was a therapy-related workshop. It was on coping with the death of a child. I'd had a miscarriage several years before, but I didn't really associate it with how I was feeling. After I read the workshop description in the catalog, I thought to myself, 'Yes, this is something I need to look into.'"

The retreat itself did help Diane to resolve the grief she'd been unconsciously carrying for a long time. "It was a very gentle process of release," she recalls. "We made small clay figures, little buddhas, and placed them among the trees and bushes in a section of the cemetery reserved for little people. It was such a simple thing, but so effective. It was as if I were making myself over again as I was molding that buddha."

Now, after a Zen training weekend, Diane feels reconstituted in other ways. "I'm not a physical person," she remarks, "and being at the monastery puts demands on you physically. But the remarkable thing is, none of those demands are more than you can handle. And I think that would be true for anyone. I didn't get much sleep the first night, but then, the next day was so stimulating that I didn't get tired. I found it too painful to sit cross-legged, so I sat in a chair. When they asked me to scrub floors, I told them about my knee surgery, and they gave me another assignment. It's a matter of doing your part to make the experience here work for you. The message here is to take charge of the things you can, and they help you here to do that."

Diane believes that the same lesson applies spiritually as well. "Thoreau claims we all lead lives of quiet desperation," she notes. "I'm sure many of the people here [for the Zen training weekend] understood this about themselves, and that's why they came. I'm one of them. You know what I said about not wanting to go to church with my friend and her mother? I used to love going to church as a kid. It was right down the block from where we lived. I'd run through the back alley to get to the service first, ahead of the rest of my family walking along the road. Now I'm starting to feel that eagerness of spirit again, that fire burning inside."

Gido: "the image became a reality"

Gido (his dharma name, meaning "way of virtue") is a monk at Zen Mountain Monastery. He's also the cook (or *tenzo*)—a traditionally very important and demanding post in a Zen monastery. Regardless of the orthodoxy associated with these roles, however, Gido himself is a true original. At age thirty, he's unusually young to be a monk, at least by Western standards, and yet he's been one for years. In fact, he took his monastic vows at Dukkoku-ji monastery in Japan not long after moving to that country from the United States at age twenty.

What prompted Gido, who was then called Paul, to make such a radical lifestyle change? As in so many cases, especially involving matters of faith, the initial stimulus was something quite small and simple. For him, it was a black-and-white photograph in a library book of a young monk seated on the porch of a Japanese zendo.

"That monk was like a rock, he was so composed," Gido remembers. "I wanted to be that person. It was an image to me of a perfected way of living, of art made practical. I wanted to know that culture, to live on that porch. As I kept dwelling on this idea, it evolved: Where can I go to live this way? Japan! But isn't it too hypermodern now? I know— a monastery!"

Gido, the cook at the monastery, stands preparing a meal at one end of a long table extending across the center of the kitchen. He wears the black tuniclike garment that monks commonly wear instead of robes outside the zendo. Within the stone archway behind him are other, larger ovens and stoves.

Gido's impulse did have a logical, positive connection to his life as a whole. The son of an art professor, he had grown up with an appreciation for aesthetics and had studied art in college. Images were therefore powerful touchstones for him, keys to accessing new levels of awareness and comprehension. "It all started out in a very romantic, intellectual way, I know," he admits. "I later realized I was crying out for some sort of grounding. I rode for a while on my fascination with the cultural aspects of Japanese Zen, but the journey ended up giving me that grounding. The image became a reality."

While Gido was still at the monastery in Japan, he read an essay written by Daido about Zen Mountain Monastery. "What Daido said regarding monasticism struck a chord with me," he recalls. "He took a basically purist, conservative approach to the subject, invoking Dogen, and yet he had a very contemporary voice. He quoted [Thomas] Merton [a twentieth-century Roman Catholic monk who had a deep appreciation of Zen] and grappled very directly with the present-day validity of being a monk. I liked that breadth of vision."

Once Gido decided to return to America, Zen Mountain Monastery was his first choice as a place to practice. "When I arrived," he remembers, "I noticed it was a beautifully cared for place, but there was also something else, an underlying spirit that felt familiar to me. It soon just swept me up. It does that every day."

As cook, Gido carries on the Zen tradition—and the monastery practice—of providing healthy, well-balanced, and well-presented meals, assisted by a daily crew of residents and guests who slice, dice, chop, mix, and perform other labor-intensive kitchen chores during the caretaking period. Occasionally a meat dish or sauce is served, much to the surprise of visitors who assume, erroneously, that Buddhists are specifically obligated by their religion not to eat meat. Most of the meals, however, are vegetarian, and if not, a vegetarian option is always available. As you might expect, the menu often features Asian dishes: for example, sushi rolls, Chinese stir-fry, miso soup, or Thai coconut curry. However, the full menu spectrum is very eclectic, as evidenced by one recent week's menu that included calzone, vichyssoise, gumbo stew, shepherd's pie, Lebanese vegetable soup, burritos, and lentil-walnut burgers.

Gido is a fine cook, but that doesn't mean he gets many compliments from the other residents. "Here they don't deal in praise," he remarks. "It runs throughout the training—the idea that you shouldn't look for approval from others, or give it to others as if you were doing them a favor. The people here are very warm and friendly, but they resist the automatic impulse to say 'good job.' It's a very purposeful withholding, definitely for your own benefit. When you think about that, it's an incredible kindness."

Gido points out that it was just the opposite in the Japanese monastery where he lived and also cooked. People there were constantly saying "good job" because, he believes, that kind of politeness is so inextricably a part of the Japanese character. He has noticed other differences as well, such as interpersonal relationships being more casual at Zen Mountain Monastery than at Dukkoku-ji monastery.

Nevertheless, Gido also finds many remarkable similarities between the two places. "From waking up through caretaking practice [the first six hours of the day], it's the same thing here that it is inside a Japanese Zen monastery," he points out. "Some people argue that American Zen should break free of all the Japanese rituals, words, and customs, but I disagree. I like the dance between Japanese and American ways that goes on here. I think the Japanese form helps the tree grow straight."

As an individual whose life embodies a unique blend of Japanese and American Zen experience, Gido now stands at another kind of crossroads. "I've only been here about seven months. I wanted to come here, I like it here, and I've taken a vow of stability that justifies my staying here. But can I give this place the level of dedication and commitment that I've come to see in the other monastics? Looking at them both inspires me and terrifies me. This place is their body and mind. Can it become mine as well? Is that what will open up for me? If not, what will?"

Hojin: "something pushing me from inside"

"I first came here in 1990 because my partner signed me up for a retreat," declares Hojin (her dharma name, meaning "dharma treasure"), one of the senior monastics at Zen Mountain Monastery. "I wasn't looking for a place to go myself." What she found, however, belied her assumption. "The experience I had at that retreat made sense of things that I'd been attracted to all my life," she says, "things that I couldn't explain but really cared about."

Hojin, then Jody, was an artist specializing in ceramics who had taught and exhibited for a number of years by the time she came to the monastery. Early in her career, she saw some Japanese pottery in which breakage and repair became part of the finished work. "I was fascinated with this concept," she says. "I wondered, where did this way of being with material come from?"

Hojin's curiosity led her to learn more about the Zen art of tea and, eventually, to enter into a ceramics apprenticeship with a Japanese teacher. Through this connection, she met a Zen priest who introduced her to zazen, which she continued to practice on her own. As the years went by, she also read books on Zen, but that's as far as it went before she found out that she'd been given the gift of a weekend at the monastery.

In preparation for that retreat, Hojin listened to some of Daido's audiotaped talks. She also obtained the latest copy of *Mountain Record*, the monastery's quarterly magazine. As soon as she saw the cover she was struck by a synchronicity: The past few days she'd been hearing the phrase "words, words, words" over and over again in her mind as she'd worked on one of her sculptures, and the *Mountain Record's* theme that issue was "Words."

After completing the weekend, Hojin felt at a loss for words to describe exactly what it was that had so captivated her about it, but she has since developed some insights. "Looking back to that time," she

Standing on the steps outside the dining hall are Daido (right) and (clockwise) Jimon, Shugen, and Hojin. Daido holds a hossu, or whisk, a symbol of dharma transmission.

recalls, "I was impressed by the energy of the people here and the depth of exploration they put into things that seemed so ordinary—the most skillful way to wash the dishes or arrange flowers in a vase or sit on a cushion. The whole emphasis on training excited me. It was similar to training in clay. I think my own training in clay helped prepare me for it. Also, because I'd once been an environmental biology major, I appreciated their interest in the environment."

Hojin later joined one of the monastery's annual wilderness explorations in the Adirondacks, led by Daido, then did a one-month residency, and shortly afterward moved into the monastery for a year. "Getting so involved with the monastery so quickly was a big challenge for me," she reveals. "I'd worked so hard to become an artist, but something else was pushing me from inside, telling me to be here full-time. It didn't really make sense to me. I wasn't too keen at first on living with a community, preferring to sit by myself, but here I was, working myself into it."

Aside from reservations about giving up her privacy, Hojin also had doubts about whether she could stay the course of the training. "I bumped up against several barriers over and over again," she admits. "Some of it had to do with what was coming up inside me during zazen. Some of it was related to working so closely with others, when I was used to working by myself."

Eventually Hojin's life at the monastery did start opening up, revealing more and more ways for her to explore and exercise her individuality. "It helped a lot that the teacher trusted me and that the others here did, too. That made me relax a bit and start trusting myself more. Also, I was feeling more alive, more clear about what I truly wanted and needed."

After two periods of lengthy residence, Hojin entered the monastic path. Currently she holds the office of program coordinator, which means that she plans the many weekend to weeklong retreats that the monastery sponsors each year. Most of them are open to the public, and all of them engage participants in following the monastic schedule. Here's a small sampling of retreats offered over the past eighteen months, to indicate their variety:

- "Knowing How to Be Satisfied": Focusing on specific texts and practices, Geoffrey Shugen Arnold, Sensei, helps retreatants examine how to pursue "middle way" lifestyles in an era of overindulgence.

- "Animal Tracking and Awareness": Jim Bruchac, naturalist and storyteller, teaches exercises and techniques for becoming more mindful in the wilderness.
- "The Landscape of American Buddhism": Richard Seegar, associate professor of Religious Studies at Hamilton College, reviews the history of Buddhism's growth in America and discusses issues involving its future.
- "Both, Both—All Ten Directions: A More Than Writing Retreat": Anne Waldman, poet and teacher at Naropa University, leads retreatants through individual and collaborative creativity and writing exercises.
- "Kendo: The Way of the Sword": Using bamboo swords and protective clothing, Sensei Noboru Kataoka of the New York Kendo Club instructs participants in the meaning and practice of this traditional Zen art.
- "Living in Harmony: The Benedictine Rule as a Model for Real Life": Sister Joan Chittister, O.S.B., discusses spiritual discipline in general and the Benedictine Rule in particular, which influenced the development of the monastic code at Zen Mountain Monastery.
- "Zen Arts Family Retreat": Working with various artistic media, senior monastics and lay students at Zen Mountain Monastery engage parents and their children in creative activities to foster deeper intimacy and communication.
- "Into White: A Winter Drawing Retreat": Hojin herself guides retreatants to investigate the sights, sounds, and smells of the natural land around the monastery and then work with traditional drawing techniques to express them.

Often Hojin talks over the phone with individuals who want to come to the monastery for retreats. "It's an incredibly diverse group," she comments. "It's very inspiring to know that so many different kinds of people are all seeking a greater sense of purpose in their lives."

3

Gates and Barriers on the Training Path

In the beginner's mind there are many possibilities;
in the expert's mind there are few.   —SHUNRYU SUZUKI

Maybe you initially come to a Zen monastery, as I did, with trepidation, having heard or read some of the hair-raising legends associated with Zen training. For example, take the sixth-century Chinese monk Hui-k'o. To convince the reluctant Bodhidharma to be his teacher, he kept steadfast vigil day after day, night after night, in knee-deep snow outside the master's refuge. When that didn't work, Hui-k'o chopped off his own right arm and presented it to Bodhidharma as a token of his seriousness. Other students in Zen history have reportedly been slapped, boxed, kicked, flagellated, shouted at, publicly humiliated, stripped of their possessions, cast out into the wilderness, and/or forced to smell rotting corpses, all for the sake of hastening their enlightenment.

On the other hand (with due apology to the one-armed Hui-k'o), perhaps you arrive at a Zen monastery for the first time anticipating hour after hour of blissful serenity in a tranquil, silent, exquisitely composed, sensorially refined environment. Tracing an altogether different pattern of images in the fabric of Zen history, you may envision all the stress of everyday life draining away as you gaze at decorous flower arrangements, inhale pine-scented incense, ponder the cosmic nature of infinity, and savor each grain of sage-infused rice that you hoist to your lips with elegantly lacquered chopsticks.

Each of these two perspectives has some validity. A Zen monastery's focus on a natural aesthetic and on fundamental activities like sitting, breathing, walking, eating, and doing elementary chores does lend any experience there a certain degree of relaxing and often inspiring simplicity. At the same time, it can be surprisingly difficult—and, accordingly, painful—to participate in this experience as thoroughly as you are asked to do.

The paradoxical situation reminds me of a famous Zen teaching tale set in ancient China, where Zen originated in the sixth century, the time of Bodhidharma, as Ch'an—a mixture of Mahayana Buddhism and native Taoism. Once an earnest seeker of wisdom undertook a long, arduous journey to consult a famous Buddhist master who lived (of course) on a remote mountaintop. When the seeker finally stood before the aged teacher, he asked him the one question that had tormented him for years: "What is the very essence of the Buddha's teaching?"

The master replied, "Do no harm. Do only good."

The seeker was furious. "That's it?" he cried. "That's what I traveled so many miles to hear? Why, any little child could have told me that!"

"Maybe so," the master responded. "It is, after all, a very simple thing to say. But it is a very hard thing to do, even for a wise, old person like myself."

Similarly, life in a Zen monastery as a visitor or a resident may be simple, but that doesn't mean it's easy. Every aspect of it is geared toward vocation—the calling to embrace one's responsibilities—rather than vacation, the act of leaving them behind.

A Zen monastery, or any other Zen training environment, is not a place to bring your favorite novels, catch up on your sleep, or dabble in

Orientalism. It is not a religious resort where you can get away from all your troubles. Instead, it's a crucible where you're encouraged at every moment to confront, examine, and take charge of what Daido calls "the whole catastrophe": your self, your life, your universe.

Buddhism is commonly misperceived as a religion that rejects the world or offers an escape from it. That may appear to be what is going on in a Zen monastery, center, or zendo. Any one of these environments is undeniably a secluded place where people spend the biggest chunk of their time sitting in silence, trying not to let their thoughts distract them.

The truth, however, is that Buddhism aims to help people become more intimately and beneficially at one with the world, so they can literally real-ize themselves, and a Zen monastery, center, or zendo is a training ground for developing the necessary skills. Chief among them is the kind of whole-minded attentiveness, concentration, and commitment that emerges through zazen.

Given the intensity of Zen practice in a communal setting (and, if you're a first-timer, the novelty of it), you will inevitably come up against your own discomforts, fears, inadequacies, and resistances. Sitting absolutely still, physically and mentally, for a thirty-five minute stretch definitely falls into the simple-not-easy category, even for veteran students. Your knees, toes, and nose can take turns screaming in pain, as your brain simultaneously broadcasts an equally maddening chorus made up of every bogeyperson from your grade-school years to your present job.

Other events in the tightly packed day can also rattle you, despite your best intentions. You may find yourself balking at having to bow and chant foreign words in a certain way for no good reason you can fathom. You may not enjoy cleaning toilets, especially in the exact manner spelled out to you by someone you disliked at first sight. You may carelessly stumble over a zabuton in the zendo and, much to your embarrassment, break the perfect rhythm of a kinhin line. And at night the snores of your dormmates—even the ones you most admired during the day—may conjure images of revenge so horrifying that you shame yourself.

At any of these grim moments, trivial though they are from an objective point of view, you may find yourself feeling tortured. Frequently you'll be told to do things that you really don't want to do, even though you know it's somehow good for you. Sometimes the message comes in the voice of your own conscience. Other times it comes in the similar sounding voice of a teacher, monk, or senior student who, like a close family member, cares enough to say "be still," "clean it up," "hurry," or "stop" without conventional politeness.

On the positive side, spending time in a Zen environment can offer uniquely wonderful moments of peace, happiness, and insight. During certain periods of sitting zazen, you may feel more physically, emotionally, and spiritually grounded than you ever have before. While chopping vegetables in the kitchen, you may discover a special pleasure and skill in doing it more mindfully under someone else's direction, rather than in your habitual and more distracted manner. As you harmonize your voice and body movements with others during services— and even as you guide yourself to sleep while others are snoring—you may sense a human interconnectedness that takes you well beyond the limiting confines of your own self-interest. And, thanks to your more keenly charged consciousness, when you pause now and then to observe a passing cloud or the glow of candlelight on polished wood or the texture of stones in a Japanese "dry" garden, something deep inside you may resonate in a way that astounds and invigorates you.

To get through the rough times and appreciate more deeply the ample occasions for joy, people new to a Zen monastery, center, or zendo can benefit enormously from what is known as "beginner's mind" (in Japanese, *shoshin*). It's the form of consciousness that allows us to enter into each experience with a fresh enthusiasm and a freedom from preconceptions, thereby keeping ourselves open to all positive outcomes possible. Zen students are urged to retain this innocent mental attitude or quality as much as they can throughout their years of practice, otherwise they risk becoming jaded, mechanical, or deadened.

Using a work-practice analogy to describe how beginner's mind functions, Daido once said, "Every weed you pull is the first weed you've ever pulled, the final weed you'll ever pull, the only weed you're going to pull in your life." This intentness on staying in the present, to the exclusion of everything else, renders each moment that occurs a new opportunity for full aliveness, undiminished by shadows of the past or the future, no matter what specific thing one may be doing at the time.

Shunryu Suzuki, the Japanese Zen master who founded San Francisco Zen Center in 1960, emphasizes the value of beginner's mind in his book *Zen Mind, Beginner's Mind*, which is still one of the most popular and instructive introductory guides to Zen. Referring to beginner's mind also as "original mind," he states:

> Our "original mind" includes everything within itself.
> It is always rich and sufficient within itself. You should
> not lose your self-sufficient state of mind. This does not
> mean a closed mind, but actually an empty mind and
> a ready mind. . . . Then we are always true to ourselves,
> in sympathy with all beings, and can actually practice.

Suzuki also argues against assuming that a person steeped in Zen knowledge has any significant advantage in Zen practice over someone who isn't—music to any newcomer's ears.

> There is no need to have a deep understanding of Zen.
> Even though you read much Zen literature, you must
> read each sentence with a fresh mind. You should not
> say, "I know what Zen is," or "I have attained enlightenment." This is also the real secret of the arts: Always
> be a beginner. Be very, very careful about this point. If
> you start to practice zazen, you will begin to appreci-

ate your beginner's mind. It is the secret of Zen practice.
(Here and above: pp. 21–22)

Let's now take a closer look at the heart of this matter: zazen. In the words of Daido, "The three most important principles of real estate are location, location, location. The three most important principles of practice are zazen, zazen, zazen."

Zazen: The Practice of Enlightenment

Zazen is sitting, plain and simple, but again, not necessarily easy. The body can prove amazingly rebellious, sometimes manifesting its restlessness in itches, twitches, or torments that seem to arise out of nowhere. Meanwhile the mind, repeatedly dubbed the "monkey mind" in Buddhist writings, can chatter on and bounce around with seemingly inexhaustible vigor, as if it were having a panic attack.

In some respects, that's exactly what's happening: Both the body and the mind are being denied their usual permission to distract, provoke, tantalize, or capture us as they will. Zazen is a person's effort to tame this beastly duo and, in doing so, realize the fundamental oneness of the self and the universe.

But even to harbor such a goal while doing zazen is to hold on to a thought and, therefore, to defeat the purpose.

From a strictly logistical perspective, zazen involves the simple act of maintaining a single, motionless body posture and letting go of all thoughts and sensations as they arise. If you sincerely apply yourself to this act, you inevitably come closer and closer to achieving a state of mental and physical stillness. The twentieth-century Zen master Taisen Deshimaru spoke of it as a clarification process: "During zazen, brain and consciousness become pure. It's exactly like muddy water left to stand in a glass. Little by little, the sediment sinks to the bottom and the water becomes pure."

By means of zazen, one becomes intimate with oneself through seeing how the mind functions and what state of being exists after all transitory thinking, feeling, and moving has ceased. This self-awareness alone does a great deal to foster wisdom about life as well as compassion toward oneself and others.

Although it's unlikely that Blaise Pascal, the seventeenth-century French philosopher, knew anything about Buddhism, he reflects the value of something like zazen in his famous maxim, "All the evil in the world comes from man's inability to sit quietly and alone in a room for a while." In our current, global society of increasingly faster-paced busyness, the type of settling down that takes place in zazen can be invaluably humanizing for each of us, man or woman, restoring our sense of wholeness and helping us perceive a larger frame of reference than our own often petty or harmful preoccupations.

From a Zen perspective, zazen has even richer significance. The process itself remains the same, but the experience of that process becomes transformative, because the mind is more spiritually attuned to engage in it.

According to Master Dogen, quoting the Buddha, zazen is not just a means of attaining enlightenment but the end in itself. In other words, zazen is the activity of an enlightened being. It was true more than twenty-five hundred years ago, when the Buddha sat underneath a tree in northern India and had his great awakening, and it's true today for anyone who sits anywhere with the serious intention to practice. Daido underscores this fact in his book *The Eight Gates of Zen.*

> The very first sitting of the rank beginner, whether properly or improperly executed, is at once the complete and perfect manifestation of the zazen of countless Buddhas and ancestors of past, present, and future. From the zazen of countless Buddhas and ancestors, our own zazen emerges. From our own zazen, the zazen of countless Buddhas and ancestors is realized. As a result, we

all live the life of Buddha, transcend Buddha, have the mind of Buddha and become Buddha. (p. 84)

Learning more about the spiritual dimension of enlightenment, the Buddha's awakening, the countless Buddhas and ancestors, or zazen ultimately requires connecting personally with a teacher, something you can usually do in various ways when you spend time in a Zen training environment. Only in this live context can you obtain the kind of information and illumination that is most vitally helpful to you as an individual. However, here are some general guidelines, similar to those commonly given at Zen monasteries, zendos, and centers, for assuming a posture and mindset that is conducive to zazen (if you have them, substitute a zafu and zabuton for a cushion and the floor):

- Sit comfortably in one of the following positions:
    - full lotus: seated on a cushion with the legs crossed in front, each foot resting on the opposite thigh;
    - half lotus: seated on a cushion with the legs crossed in front, one foot (either one) resting on the opposite thigh, the other foot on the floor;
    - Burmese: seated on a cushion with the legs crossed in front, both feet resting next to each other on the floor, close to the body;
    - *seiza:* kneeling with a cushion or bench supporting the buttocks;
    - sitting in a chair with the feet flat on the floor and the back away from the back of the chair (this last option is available in many Zen institutions, including Zen Mountain Monastery, but not all. If you're concerned about whether chair use is possible at a place you want to visit, check in advance).
- Clasp the hands loosely together at the waist. In many places the standard zazen *mudra* ("hand position" in Sanskrit) is made by laying the left fingers on top of the right and touching the thumbs together above them, so that a

hollow O is formed by the linked thumbs and the stacked fingers.

- Looking downward, leave the eyes slightly open and unfocused rather than closing them, which can lead to sleep or chaotic imagery.
- When a thought or sensation arises, acknowledge it and then gently let it go.

As a means of extending and enhancing the clarity, attentiveness, and self-awareness developed through zazen, most Zen institutions offer a range of other, more or less formal activities to practice. At Zen Mountain Monastery, Daido has created and implemented a uniquely comprehensive training matrix called the Eight Gates of Zen, delineated in his book of the same name (quoted above). In addition to zazen, the gates include Zen study, academic study, liturgy, right action, art practice, body practice, and work practice. All these gates are outlined by Daido in his foreword to this book.

The Eight Gates program is not offered elsewhere. However, because of its all-inclusive nature, I can use it here as a framework for discussing different Zen-related activities that may also be available in various forms at other monasteries, centers, and zendos. Each of the remaining seven gates is described separately below.

Zen Study: The Teacher-Student Relationship

Buddhism is not a religion of the book or of revealed truth, as are, for example, Christianity, Judaism, and Islam. It is a religion whose truths can be discovered only within oneself through personal experience, and the only reliable guide in such an endeavor is a person who has been officially acknowledged as a master of it: a teacher. For the student, this person becomes a living representative of the great teacher himself, the Buddha.

Zen is perhaps the purest expression in Buddhism of this key principle. Its teachings have been passed down—mind to mind—from teacher to student since the beginning of its history, so that each school has its own, distinct ancestral lineage. Therefore, the teacher-student relationship has persisted for centuries as the linchpin of Zen transmission, and personal study with an authentic teacher continues to be critical to Zen training.

Apart from the traditional argument for a teacher, there's also the purely rational one. You can get a lot of information about Zen on your own, but you can't stand outside of yourself and evaluate how well or poorly you understand it or actualize it in your life. Only a qualified teacher can help you to do that.

At Zen Mountain Monastery, up to three teachers are available at any one time to give instruction to residents and retreatants. This happens in a number of ways, according to the daily, weekly, monthly, and seasonal monastic schedule. Among them are:

- formal talk (dharma discourse/talk or *teisho*)
- informal question-and-answer discussion (*mondo*)
- private, face-to-face teaching encounter (dokusan or, if not with an abbot, *daisan*)
- public, one-on-one teaching encounter (dharma combat or *sosan*)
- casual interaction during the course of living, working, and eating together

I describe some of these teaching modes more thoroughly in chapter 4.

Many Zen institutions offer similar Zen study opportunities. However, the number of available teachers varies from place to place and some may not provide one, which would eliminate all of the above options. Others do not offer communal life with a sangha, which could restrict or rule out the more public forms of teaching. For questions to ask a particular Zen monastery, center, or zendo on these issues and others discussed below, see chapter 6.

Academic Study: Buddhist Writings and Ideas

Although Buddhism is not a religion of the book, it has produced a wealth of writings, from sutras believed to convey the words of the Buddha himself to commentaries, historical records, and texts pursuing philosophical, psychological, or sociocultural themes. Examining these writings helps to condition the student's mind for practice. It also deepens his or her appreciation of the traditions that have kept Buddhism in general and Zen in particular vital for so many centuries and that are crucial to their survival in the West.

These works are often officially assigned for supervised or private study during various times of the year as well as during progressive stages in an individual student's training. For example, at Zen Mountain Monastery, during each *ango* season (a period of intensified practice: March through May in the spring and September through November in the fall) the entire sangha investigates a different section of the *Shobogenzo: The Treasury of the Dharma Eye*. This seminal work by the great Japanese Zen master Eihei Dogen (1200–1253) is widely considered to be not only the most significant collection of Zen commentaries but also a masterpiece in world literature. Within each ango season, a full week, open to retreatants, is spent intensively reviewing and discussing different translations and interpretations of the section under Daido's direct guidance.

In addition, Zen Mountain Monastery periodically sponsors weekend programs that focus on a specific work or on the writings of a particular master. Other Zen institutions also offer these kinds of events as well as their own specialized forms of academic study.

A view of the front half, north side, of the zendo shows three rows of students and visitors. To the right is the carpeted rioban and the altar. Designated laypeople stand on the rioban's north side, monastics on the south (not seen). Here the officiant stands in the middle, before a kneeling mat, with two attendants behind him.

Liturgy: Making Visible the Invisible

Every religion has its own ceremonial activities that encapsulate and express its core values and inspire participants to embrace them. The main elements of Zen liturgy are chanting and bowing, both of which provide a person with the symbolic experience of embodying the dharma. For Zen students (and in some places, retreatants for a month or longer), liturgical practice may also include filling a service position, such as usher, instrumentalist, or attendant to the officiant, who is usually a teacher or senior student.

In a Zen institution, liturgical chanting and bowing can take place during a variety of ceremonial occasions. Among them are formal daily services (for example, in the morning, at noon, and in the evening); invocational preludes to daily communal activities like eating, working, or assembling for a talk; and/or during special weekly, monthly, or seasonal observances.

The purpose of Zen liturgy is not to worship anyone or anything but to unite in oneness with others and with the path of enlightenment. Much of it doesn't make sense on a strictly logical level, which accounts for why many people initially resist it. Instead, it's an immediate, ritualized way to transcend the limits of rationality, individuality, and secularity. Practicing liturgy is manifesting the invisible, the intangible, the intuitive, the inherently perfect. The more you refine that practice, the clearer the manifestation becomes.

Liturgy is especially powerful in a group setting because it brings people together in spirit as well as in body. When one bows, it is a humbling (or, in the case of a full bow, quite literally a grounding) of the self. The bower is not venerating a god but honoring the buddha nature he or she shares with everyone else, as taught by the Buddha himself and reflected in his life. The same kind of oneness is communicated by bringing the palms together in the *gassho* gesture.

Chanting also helps alter a person's state of consciousness from an ego-based frame of reference to one that is more in tune with other people and, through them, with the universe at large. Whatever is actually being chanted, the chanter is giving him- or herself to the common voice. The material context for this offering may be a religious scripture (a sutra or a *gatha,* which is a short verse), a list of spiritual ancestors, or a litany of sounds without any rational meaning (a *dharani*). Some of the chants intoned on a daily basis at Zen Mountain Monastery are printed in appendix C at the end of this book.

In most Zen environments, liturgical services and invocations are orchestrated by a variety of traditional bells and drums. The latter may include the wondrously resonant and curiously shaped *mokugyo* instrument. Resembling a portly sea creature (the meaning of the Japanese name), its wooden body emits a big, hollow *thock* sound through its slightly open mouth when its back is struck with a padded wooden stick.

Although the instrumentation as a whole is pleasantly exotic to the Western ear, it's meant to signal the order and pace of events rather than provide musical accompaniment to them. Distinct sounds are assigned to each function. The mokugyo, for example, is only played to establish the rhythm during each chant. Certain bell rings are used exclusively to indicate a standing bow, as opposed to others that indicate a full bow to the floor. In other Zen places a different combination of bells and wooden instruments may be used to set the rhythm of chanting and bowing.

Just as the instrumentation helps ensure that all the participants act in unison, so do the customary practices of chanting in monotone, maintaining the same standing posture, and, if books are used, holding them in the identical manner. Like the relative uniformity in dress, these conventions assist each individual to center his or her attention on the present moment, escape preoccupation with self, and unite more easily with others.

In many Zen places, especially monasteries, you are also implicitly expected to keep your eyes to yourself during services and invocations. To look around is to function as a spectator rather than a participant. Aside from distracting others, it inevitably short-circuits your own engagement in the liturgical process and, as a result, its power to recharge your spirit.

At the same time, however, you need to keep yourself sensitive to what is happening around you, if only to stay in harmony with the event's choreography and to discover what is implicitly expected of you. An old Japanese saying articulates the requirement well: "Don't look, but see everything."

A zoologist and fellow student at Zen Mountain Monastery once described this act to me as the way animals naturally use their vision. Whenever they're undertaking some important task, he claimed, they can simultaneously focus their attention on the central matter and expand their field of peripheral awareness. Perhaps because our own deepest biological instincts incline us toward the same skill, it's a surprisingly easy and satisfying one to develop over time. It also proves helpful in every other aspect of Zen practice or, for that matter, life itself.

Right Action: Moral and Ethical Engagement in Life

In every form of Buddhism, including Zen, core precepts serve as guidelines for leading a moral and ethical existence—or, as it's often called in Zen, the life of a buddha. The official number of precepts and their specific wording differs from school to school and place to place, but they always include at least the following five precepts (expressed here in one widely used formulation):

1. Avoid causing harm to other sentient beings.
2. Avoid taking anything that is not freely given.
3. Avoid sexual misconduct.

4. Avoid untruthfulness.

5. Avoid clouding the mind with drugs.

For the precepts adopted at Zen Mountain Monastery, see page 176.

The precepts are similar in content to the ten commandments in the Bible, but they function somewhat differently. Instead of being *directives* from a higher power that one obeys from the start, they are *intentions* that one takes up and, in the process of awakening to the self and the universe, gradually learns how to incorporate more and more vitally into one's life. While the former are appropriate for a theistic religion, the latter are more in keeping with a teacher-based religion.

Precepts are recited as vows on becoming a Buddhist (in Zen, during a Jukai ceremony) and on being ordained as a monastic (in Zen, during a *tokudo* ceremony, which typically features a larger number of precepts). Otherwise, they serve as principles of thought, speech, and behavior that can be—and, for Buddhists, should be—invoked, enacted, and examined throughout one's day-to-day life. They inform the basic codes of conduct at Zen monasteries, centers, and zendos and are occasionally the subject of talks, workshops, and retreats held at these institutions.

Another dimension of right action in a Buddhist context involves social and environmental outreach: special efforts to extend wisdom and compassion into areas and populations that critically need such intervention. At Zen Mountain Monastery, students help conduct programs with prisoners, senior citizens on assisted care, and people living with HIV/AIDS. The monastery also offers retreats open to the public that bring participants into closer contact with homeless people (for example, as their hosts at a banquet-style holiday dinner each December) and with the natural world (for example, during annual "Born as the Earth" wilderness explorations in the Adirondack Mountains). Other Zen monasteries, centers, and zendos sponsor their own social-action programs and retreats. For example, the San Francisco Zen Center operates a hospice, and the Cambridge Zen Center (Massachusetts) operates an outreach program to young people at local colleges.

Art Practice: Zen and the Creative Process

During the period when Zen flourished most strongly in Japan (roughly 800 to 1700 CE), it permeated every aspect of Japanese culture. In turn, Japanese culture influenced Zen to express itself in all sorts of new ways. The result was the evolution of many refined art practices through which one can cultivate and experience different aspects of Zen sensibility, including a regard for simplicity, intimacy, naturalness, spontaneity, and whole mind-and-body focus. The arts that convey these characteristics and are considered distinctively Zen include the following:

- *brush painting and calligraphy:* the fully-engaged process of tapping and releasing energy to create an especially powerful composition
- *chado:* the way of tea (which includes the tea ceremony), involving grace and ceremony in both the preparation of tea and the tea-partaking interchange between host and guest
- *haiku:* a seventeen-syllable poem (in three lines of 5-7-5) capturing the essence of a subject
- *ikebana:* the arrangement of flowers in a spiritually and aesthetically satisfying manner
- *Noh drama:* a style of theater aimed at the direct communication of experience and emotion
- *pottery making:* a naturalistic approach to making pottery that conveys singular respect for the materials and the process
- *shakuhachi:* the playing of a bamboo flute in harmony with the breath and the emotional force moving the breath

A Zen arts retreat leader plays the shakuhachi, a traditional Japanese bamboo flute, at the back of the zendo (rarely used for such purposes). The large bell hanging from the hallway beam is the densho, struck during services.

■ *Zen gardening:* a meditative approach to creating, tending, and enjoying a garden

In addition to featuring the designated Zen arts in special talks, exhibitions, and retreats, some Zen institutions incorporate them into their regular schedules. They may reserve daily or weekly times for residents and guests to engage in supervised art practice. Zen Mountain Monastery, for instance, offers two or three such sessions each week during ango. The rest of the year, temporary residents staying at the monastery for a week or a month can pursue their own art practice during weekday afternoons.

More commonly among Zen institutions, the Zen arts are woven into the fabric of ongoing life rather than practiced individually in any sort of formal way. Flowers on an altar or even a side table are usually arranged according to principles of ikebana. A permanent Zen garden on the premises can function not only as a constant source of inspiration but also as a recurring work assignment. Zen pottery, brush painting, and calligraphy throughout the facility may subtly condition one's mind to be more open to enlightenment or at least to the experience of the moment. So may the occasional sound of someone playing a shakuhachi during a break.

A number of Zen organizations widen their exploration of the creative process to include contemporary or Western art forms, which can also serve as valuable tools for discovering the self and awakening to spirituality. Looking through recent newsletters and brochures from a variety of Zen places, I've seen programs open to the public on sculpting, journal writing, storytelling, free verse composition, improvisational theater, and turning found objects into musical instruments.

At Zen Mountain Monastery, Daido periodically offers a weeklong "mindful photography" retreat. Although it derives strength from his personal expertise, it's not meant to teach specific skills but, rather, to strip away an individual's photography-related conditioning. He or she can then "see" with a camera more intuitively and become more at one with the photographic endeavor. Because of this approach to its subject, the retreat is equally beneficial for experts *and* beginners as well as everyone in between, which makes it ideal for art practice in a Zen environment.

Body Practice: Whole Being Aliveness

Besides certain art forms, there are also specific body practices that have come to be classified as Zen ways. They evolved similarly and simultaneously in Japan, but their roots go back even earlier to China, where Zen originated under the Chinese name Ch'an. That's when traveling monks were first compelled by the dangers of the road and the principles of their path to battle opponents with a maximum of skill and a minimum of harm. Among these practices are the following:

Daido leads a discussion at one of his periodic weeklong retreats at the monastery, "Seeing with the Unconditioned Eye: Mindful Photography."

- *aikido:* a dynamic defensive activity involving body movement and sparring with a short staff or small sword (*aiki*) to avoid injury
- *jujitsu, judo, karate, and kung-fu:* different kinds of martial arts in which one uses only one's body, working in harmony with the opponent's posture and energy, to render the opponent harmless
- *kendo:* the way of the sword, generally taught with a bamboo sword and protective clothing
- *kyudo:* a form of archery combining spiritual and physical training

Zen places that sponsor a wide range of retreats or special programs tend to include these practices in the mix. They may also offer other systems of mental-plus-physical exercise that are gentler and noncombative in nature: from traditional ones, such as tai-chi, *nei-kung, qigong,* and yoga, to contemporary ones based on various physical fitness routines or on more creative, freestyle body movements.

Regularly engaging in such activities can be helpful in practicing Zen because they build up one's energy or life force (in Japanese, *ki;* in Chinese, *ch'i*), which, during zazen, helps develop dynamic mind power (in Japanese, *joriki*). For this reason, many Zen institutions add them to their daily or weekly schedule or provide space and time for people to do them on their own.

Work Practice: The Sacredness of Labor

Zen is unique among all schools of Buddhism in placing a strong emphasis on work. This tradition allegedly began with the eighth-century Ch'an master Pai-chang. Rejecting the already age-old monastic custom of simply begging for a living, he taught his monks to combine a zazen mentality with daily labor in the monastery and its surrounding fields. As a result, the monks and their master made themselves self-sufficient and better able to appreciate the universal applicability of their practice.

According to legend, one day Pai-chang's monks, convinced that their beloved teacher had become too old and feeble to work, secretly took his gardening tools and hid them away. After unsuccessfully pleading for their return, Pai-chang simply refused to eat, saying, "No work, no food."

Continuing this philosophy today, Zen Mountain Monastery and many other Zen monasteries, centers, and zendos typically schedule regular caretaking periods during which everyone present assists in doing maintenance chores with the same kind of silent, single-minded intensity that they're asked to bring to zazen. In addition, monastics and long-term residents in some of these places, including Zen Mountain Monastery, have ongoing work assignments that they strive to fulfill with the same kind of effort.

Americans in particular are inclined by their culture to fear, demean, dislike, or otherwise discount work, despite the fact that it takes up a

Participants gather in the big meadow in back of the monastery's main building for a kyudo retreat. Kyudo is the way of the bow, one of the traditional Zen arts. At the monastery, it's considered a form of body practice.

large portion of one's waking time. Speaking as just such an American, I know that working in a Zen environment with the type of whole-hearted commitment it inspires can be an incredible learning experience. It helps one to see work anywhere as a spiritual activity rather than an all-too-worldly scourge, grind, or shtick. As the expression goes: "To a secular mentality, nothing seems sacred; to a sacred mentality, everything does."

Another dimension of work practice is "right livelihood," which, like "right action," is a part of the Noble Eightfold Path taught by the Buddha (for a list of all eight parts, see the glossary entry "Eightfold Path, Noble"). Right livelihood entails not only extending our practice of mindfulness into our job or profession but also making sure that the type of work we do nourishes others rather than harming them. The latter challenge can become quite complicated given the current cut-throat nature of the marketplace and the moral ambiguity surrounding countless issues in law, medicine, education, government, the media, and other sectors of public life.

Many Zen institutions provide guidance on such matters through talks, seminars, and retreats. Sometimes these events focus on specific kinds of careers, like being a health-care professional, a corporate employee, or an artist. Other times they revolve around topics relating to work in general, such as finding new ways to exercise compassion or creating a workplace code of ethics.

Gates and Barriers: Personal Testimony

The gates to Zen training that I've just described may be compelling in print, and there's no doubt that they can each lead to wonderful, life-transforming experiences. However, when we actually take up Zen practice, these gates can sometimes loom as barriers rather than portals to spiritual development.

What can turn a gate into a barrier? In certain situations the problem may seem a definitive one, beyond our capability of changing: a physical, emotional, or psychological block that feels insurmountable; concepts or directions that defy comprehension; tasks that appear too difficult, disagreeable, or pointless to do. Then, as we take up the Zen challenge of becoming one with that barrier rather than separating from it, we can engineer a miracle: The barrier can turn into a gate.

Often in Zen training a teacher points out the way. Bonnie Myotai Treace, Sensei (Myotai being her dharma name, meaning "wondrous, subtle truth"), is the vice-abbess of Zen Mountain Monastery and the spiritual leader of its affiliate, Zen Center of New York City. She received full dharma transmission from Daido in 1996, thereby becoming his first dharma successor and a teacher in her own right after thirteen years of training. In 1998 she gave a talk entitled "Dogen Cubed" that triggered a breakthrough for me in coming to understand the writings of Dogen.

At the time, I was storming a barrier posed by the "Sounds of the Valley Streams" section from Dogen's *Shobogenzo*. It read like gibberish to me, and yet it was a key part of what experts have long regarded as a literary and spiritual masterpiece. It was also the core text in my academic study for ango. I found it intolerable that I—a former college English instructor, a writer by trade, and a sentient being now on fire with religious zeal—just didn't get it.

Myotai prefaced her talk by describing the familiar puzzle in visual perspective known as Necker's cube. It's a drawing of two overlapping squares whose corresponding corners are connected, so that when you look at the total image, you alternately see two different cubes fluctuating in a disturbing manner that never settles down. She went on to draw the analogy that fell so effectively on my prepared ears.

> This [looking at Necker's cube] strikes me as similar to
> studying the teachings of Master Dogen, where he often
> forces an oscillation of consciousness between what we

During caretaking practice, a resident and two retreatants spruce up a dry (one with a bed of small stones) Zen garden.

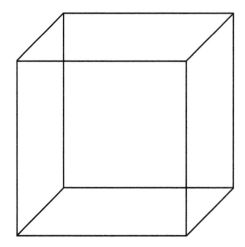

first may think is obvious and superficial with what feels deeper and more sacred. As soon as our understanding begins to rest in any interpretation, the top sinks, the bottom rises.

Later in the talk, Myotai connected the Necker's cube analogy to Zen practice as a whole.

> When we try to fix the nature of what is real, that fixing creates an enormous and unnecessary tension, imprisoning the moment within the bars of an idea. . . . There is another way. We need only to look again at the oscillating cube, the path and the perfection. In that moment the unstoppable, unbounded energy of sacred activity manifests as this life. Our work consists of simply not looking away. (Here and above: as reprinted in *Mountain Record*, fall 1998, pp. 13–19)

As far as my Dogen study was concerned, this nudge led me to stop imposing my particular intellectual demands on the section. I realized that they were only preventing it from functioning more dynamically in my mind. Once I began suspending judgment on the words and attending them more intimately, both in my study and in my life, the section started opening up for me. A reputed gate that I'd experienced as a barrier became a gate in reality.

Since that incident, I've also associated the Necker's cube analogy with the whole concept of gates being barriers and barriers being gates. It's a perceptual shift that one is encouraged to make—and that happens gradually or spontaneously—again and again in Zen practice.

Let's now consider what other people associated with Zen Mountain Monastery have to say about their own practice, and some of the gates and barriers they have encountered along the way.

Troy: *"finding that mind-body ease"*

When Troy first phoned Zen Mountain Monastery from his home in Alaska, his enthusiasm was sky high. He'd been sitting zazen on his own for a year. He'd loved his Japanese religion class in college. He'd decided to stay at the monastery at least a month.

The senior monastic on the other end of the line brought Troy back down to earth. "No one had ever asked me the questions about my life that she did," he recalls. "They went straight to my heart. Five minutes into the call, I was a wreck."

Troy's interviewer, cautioning him that his notions about Zen might be "overly romantic," told him he could come for a week, and then they'd have to see about extending his residency. He laughs about it now: "I wanted to say, 'It will take me longer to get there than you're letting me stay,' but I didn't. I was sure I'd be there for the full month."

Troy liked his life at Zen Mountain Monastery right away. "It was exactly what I was looking for," he remembers. "I'm the type of person that really thrives on the kind of rigor here. The discipline of zazen suits me. So does working with my hands, and I get many chances here to do that."

Comparing his early experience at the monastery to his years as a wrestler, Troy says, "Like wrestling, which is an individual sport, it

Flanking John Daido Loori, Roshi, are his transmitted students, Bonnie Myotai Treace, Sensei (left); and Geoffrey Shugen Arnold, Sensei. Myotai and Shugen belong to the second generation of American Zen teachers. Daido is part of the first generation, trained by Asian teachers. American Zen monks customarily shave their heads for their ordination (tokudo) but, depending on the rule of their order, may choose not to do so afterward.

required a lot of determination, a lot of pushing myself hard. I felt I could do anything I wanted, I simply had to do it myself. It wasn't about relying on other people but jumping in on my own."

Troy did wind up staying at the monastery for a month, during which he applied himself very intensely to practice. "I would go early to sit and stay late. I found the mystery of it so engaging. Here I was, actually doing it!" Soon, however, he began having palpable symptoms that he might be overdoing it. "One day I was so tense that I said to Daido, 'I feel as if I swallowed a bowling ball.' He told me, 'You need to relax. Just relax.'"

Troy went home for a while but later returned to the monastery for a yearlong residency. Again he immediately sensed he was where he belonged and had the best opportunity for realizing himself. Nevertheless, by the end of the year he was feeling so pressured and backed into a corner by his practice that he was becoming physically ill. "I knew

I had to loosen up a bit," he says, "but I couldn't figure out how to do that, so I just left for a while."

Now Troy is back, and there's much less anxiety. "I have learned how to relax more," he explains. "Much of the pain before came from moving away from things I didn't want to see in myself. The same thoughts would come up over and over again, trying to lead me down a path that I knew would make me uncomfortable, and I would ignore those thoughts, so the pain was manifesting itself physically. Now that I'm aware of the pattern, I can see it coming and begin to relax more, so it's less of a problem. I think finding that mind-body ease in practice can take a long time. At least it did for me."

One area that Troy still wrestles with is liturgy. "To this day," he claims, "one of the hardest things for me is the chanting. The sound of my voice is horrible to me. It's as if I'm afraid of it, or afraid of expressing myself. I'm not a big talker, and I can get so self-conscious listening to myself when I chant that I feel my heart pounding."

Service positions, which require taking a formal role in public ceremonies, are similarly daunting to Troy. "All my nerves are on the surface," he admits. "I'm so worried about screwing up. The training [for the positions] appears to be so minimal before you have to begin. Actually it isn't, it's very thorough, but it's perfectly concise. You have to learn how to really listen and take it in, instead of just being too scared by it to focus."

Finally, there's the off-the-record barrier/gate of social interaction. "I've always been a private person with a very small circle of friends," Troy says. "Living in a community like the one at the monastery can sometimes be difficult. To me, there's a surprising amount of time when people are just talking informally with each other. For some reason, I didn't expect there would be that much socializing in a Zen environment. Sometimes it's hard for me to talk with people at meals. I've been told I put up a block, and I know there's some truth to that. It took a while until I found a few people I could really confide in."

Reflecting on his training so far at the monastery, Troy remarks, "All the things you've thought about yourself are going to be hung up on a billboard for you to look at, and it's a sobering experience! It takes place all the time, not just in zazen. And occasionally other people will do the looking for you and let you know about it, one way or the other. But then a wonderful thing starts happening. It's like when you first start driving a car—all of a sudden your life begins changing. There's more movement, there's more you can do."

Asked to describe his own personal transformation more specifically, Troy responds, "Before I came here, I didn't think there was any hope for much difference in my life. I thought I was already pretty much who I was going to be. Maybe I'd get smarter as I got older, but my basic self wasn't going to develop all that much beyond where it was. Now there seems to be so much more possibility in my life. I also see other people differently. I used to think there were just certain kinds of people. Now I see each individual more compassionately, and I can let that individual into myself more."

Jimon: "how to bring it alive"

Before coming to Zen Mountain Monastery in the mid-1980s, Jimon (her dharma name, meaning "gate of compassion") toured as a lead soloist and rehearsal director for the world-famous Nikolais Dance Theatre. Her extraordinarily successful career brought her many moments of ecstasy as a dancer but, apart from them, an increasingly greater amount of suffering as a human being. She writes candidly about the dilemma in a 1994 *Mountain Record* article:

> The more recognition I received, the more I needed. It was a vicious cycle that never satisfied me or offered any peace, and yet this was the only place I felt alive. Eventually, the vacancy of this life became intolerable, and

the courage to step out from under the spotlight and off of the stage began to replace the terror of living the rest of my life as a addicted ghost. . . . I learned so much [as a performer], and had many wonderful experiences which I will never forget. What was not so wonderful, though, was my persistent preoccupation with myself as I tried to fill the emptiness I felt inside.

Against all worldly logic advanced by her own mind and by concerned loved ones, Jimon gave up her life as a professional dancer to become monastic. She celebrates the result in the same article:

Nothing I have ever done has so challenged who I believe myself to be or not to be. It's allowed me to access the kind of generosity I thought others embodied but somehow was deficient in me. The feeling of full-heartedness is incomparable. No amount of applause or approval has come close to its power to continually heal and nourish myself as well as others. (Here and above: "The Irrational Heart," *Mountain Record,* winter 1994, pp. 32–35)

Surprisingly, one of the most significant challenges Jimon has faced in her fifteen years at the monastery has been art practice—even when she has chosen dance as her medium, which she has often done. "Looking back," she confides, "I can see that my first art practice stuff was awful. I came to the monastery feeling very confident about my creative abilities, but it's obvious to me now that I didn't really know or enter into what art practice is about. I kept relying on the same tricks or gimmicks I'd learned as a professional to get me through. Rather than letting go and trusting myself, I was ripping myself off from the opportunity to truly study myself."

Jimon estimates that she floundered along for "seven or eight years" feeling she was good at art practice and didn't need to put a great deal of effort into it but, at the same time, realizing that she wasn't getting much out of it and didn't quite grasp how to do so. Finally she made what she calls the "terrifying decision" to find out. She dropped the facade of being an artist and, along with it, any investment in a "good idea" or an "impressive outcome." She cast aside whatever notions might arise in her mind of getting, grasping, or giving. Instead, she just did the practice.

For Jimon, this approach to creativity continues to be a matter—once again—of doing something simple but not easy. According to her, it's also a difficult thing to describe in words, because it reveals itself only in process. She speaks of it indirectly as the act of uncovering the truth that's already there. "Art practice is pointing at not dressing things up but stripping things away," she says. "Can you get to the very essence of it all? Can you express it with the least amount of fanciness? It's like what you do to yourself in zazen: pulling all the crap away, seeing what remains, and being prepared to let others see it, too."

Jimon's involvement with liturgy at the monastery has followed an altogether different route toward the same kind of understanding. For most of her monastic career, she has been liturgy master, a position that makes her the principal leader of chanting during services and invocations. "Right from the beginning," she maintains, "I have always received a lot from the chanting. It has kept opening up and opening up for me as long as I've been practicing it."

On a very basic level, Jimon, who has no background as a musician, compares this evolution to what she assumes happens in the course of learning how to sing or play an instrument: One puts more and more of one's body into it, and the body then responds more and more wholeheartedly. As time goes by, the activity develops into a means of recharging oneself. "When I'm tired and put myself into the chanting," she notes, "whoa, does the energy come!"

On a higher level, Jimon describes the ongoing reward of chanting in terms of the collective spiritual energy it can generate. "It's what occurs when everyone's voice comes together so there's one sound," she explains. "You lose any separate awareness of yourself chanting. It's more than a harmony, it's an intimacy with everyone and everything. The zendo feels like the center of the universe."

Both as the liturgy master and as a single voice, Jimon strives to make this phenomenon happen whenever the sangha gathers to chant. She tells herself, "Okay, so it's my five hundredth service. The question is still how to bring it alive. That is my mission, every single time."

Referring specifically to her role as chant leader during a service, Jimon says that she works to create a mutual exchange of energy among herself and the two other major elements involved—the percussionist and the sangha—so that no one of them is merely leading or following. "When I first got the assignment," she recalls, "I approached it gung ho, forcing everyone to go along exactly at my pace. The effect was pretty lifeless, so I tried the other extreme, following their pace, which inevitably got slower and slower until the chanting sounded like a dirge. The solution lay in creating a relationship much like a dance in which the partners are so intimate that they move each other. You can't really tell who the leader is."

Recently Jimon completed a long period of also being work master. She'd been chosen for the assignment in part because a senior monastic had never held it and, therefore, brought to it his or her more experienced understanding of work as a Zen practice. She knew very little, however, about the nitty-gritty, practical stuff involved in the job. "When I took over as work master," she admits, "I was filled with fear. I was worried that I'd be humiliated, that people would look at me with no respect."

At first Jimon couldn't get past this insecurity. When she wasn't certain how to go about handling a project, she usually backed off and allowed someone else to take over. "I was holding on to my fear," she admits, "rather than letting go of it, staying with the project, and learning about it." These early experiences were especially galling to her because of her keen awareness that work practice in Zen is not about doing well but about being open to work and engaging in it with a beginner's mind.

Finally Jimon defeated what she'd come to call "the monster in my head" and put herself into each work task that came along. The effect was amazingly affirmative. "I found out so much that's exciting about work," she says, "and so much that I didn't know about myself. The whole experience showed me my weaknesses very glaringly, but it also revealed a surprising part of me that really wants to learn, that really wants to know how to do things."

4

The Weekly Schedule: Being in the Moment

When you find your place where you are, practice occurs.

—MASTER DOGEN

The first time I saw the Pacific Ocean, I was overwhelmed. I'd just driven overnight through the desert along the Mexican border. I'd parked my car at the bottom of a tall, sandy ridge, climbed up to the top, and there it was, suddenly, surprisingly, and all at once: long, straight combers from horizon to horizon, rolling in to hit the far side of a broad, empty beach. The feeling that shot through me then had no distinguishable parts: I couldn't tell whether it was mental or physical, terrifying or thrilling, temporary or permanent.

Whatever it was, it prompted me immediately to scramble down the hundred-foot slope, dash across the beach, shuck off my clothes, and dive into the ocean, as if my salvation were at stake. Once immersed in the powerfully rolling water, I instinctively did what was necessary, and also what I'd been taught to do as a child learning to swim in the Atlantic: I gave myself up to the energy of the ocean. I knew without thinking that I had to move with it, rather than against it, to survive.

Hindsight now tells me something more. I probably also knew without thinking that I had to dive into the ocean right away or else I'd be too intimidated to do so for who knows how long. At some level I may have realized that not responding to such a pure feeling would result in a kind of death.

My first encounter with life at Zen Mountain Monastery was comparable in nature. Although not quite as dramatic as my personal discovery of the Pacific in 1967, it presented the same, psychical life-or-death challenge. I could definitely sense the energy being generated by the community, and I knew in my head and heart that I had to throw myself into it: not only to get through the retreat but also to reanimate something dead in the way I was living.

Before engaging in Zen practice, I'd always been skeptical of the notion of "energy" in any sort of spiritual context. I went along with it publicly—who was I to disagree with my Woodstock Generation peers?—but privately I considered it delusional. Yes, one could be turned on or off by certain people, places, things, or activities, but to me it was a matter of intellectual or biochemical mood swings rather than metaphysical energy vibes.

My first weekend living at Zen Mountain Monastery changed my mind. Since then, every period I've stayed there has had the same effect. When I allow myself to be present in the moment-by-moment schedule and give up my prickly, recalcitrant self to join the community at large, I sometimes undeniably sense a renewal of energy. The experience is probably much like the chant recharging that Jimon describes (see chapter 3). My self is invigorated as well as expanded. Instead of being confined by the skin bag and mind frame I normally call "me," it feels liberated and limitless.

Then the energy wanes, and my rational mind, off on its own again, immediately starts distrusting that such energy ever existed. I know, however, that I did sense it, and this knowledge counts.

It is said that the three essential elements in Zen practice are great faith, great doubt, and great determination. The "great doubt" part involves never fearing to challenge your faith with questions, rather than subscribing to it blindly, defiantly, or subserviently. I can't say that my skepticism about energy has been banished altogether, but I now believe in it about as often as I don't—an ebb and flow that has given my life much greater vitality. I regard my ambivalence about this matter as an element of my "great doubt," and I'm grateful that the monastery provides a place to work with it so directly and constructively.

Another significant Buddhist concept relating to this issue is symbolized by the Diamond Net of Indra. It's an image that Buddhism borrowed from Hinduism (Indra being the supreme Hindu god) and invested with its own special meaning. The net represents the universe. At each of its intersections is a diamond that reflects every other diamond in the net. A more penetrating look reveals that each diamond exists only because of the presence of all the others. What's more, within each diamond the replication process continues ad infinitum.

Symbolically, the image of the Diamond Net of Indra conveys the interdependence of all things, including every self, so that each single part contains the whole, much like any single piece you break off a hologram. I interpret this image to mean, among other things, that we derive our energy and life from the entire universe and that we are correspondingly responsible to it and for it. The notion of a separate self is only a convenient illusion, necessary in a practical way for leading a life in this world of linear time and three-dimensional space. Beyond this illusion, however, we are all one reality. We can occasionally sense this truth—often as life-affirming energy—when we make the effort to do so.

Living in a Zen environment, even if only for a few days, can yield this kind of experience and insight. To obtain it, however, you need to enter into that life with your whole body and mind.

The traditional schedule of a Zen monastery in particular follows a finely honed pattern that has fostered and reinforced such spiritual enlightenment for centuries. Nevertheless, no matter how worthwhile that schedule is or how self-disciplined you're determined to be, it would be unrealistic to expect yourself to sustain total engagement in each and every moment of it. From what I've heard, that's a daunting challenge even for long-term monastics. Instead, the point is not to let yourself stay stuck in resisting, rejecting, or standing apart from the matter at hand. When that happens, your practice is to guide your attention gently back to the here and now.

Also, in addition to the schedule itself, it's important to bear in mind something that is equally if not more valuable: the spirit of the sangha around you, a community of people who, in myriad ways, share your quest, your universe, and your very self. Participating effectively in life at a monastery entails cooperating with them, which helps you to realize both the smallness and the vastness of yourself.

To give you a better nuts-and-bolts understanding of what life in a Zen monastery is like, I'm first going to usher you hour by hour through a typical weekday at Zen Mountain Monastery during spring ango (March through May). The journey itself will *not* be typical but, rather, personal and impressionistic, based on an actual Wednesday I spent there. My intention is to leave plenty of blank space in your image of life at a Zen monastery to fill with your own experiences should you eventually wind up in one yourself.

The schedule we'll be following below is the same for any normal Tuesday (after 2:00 P.M.) through Saturday during spring ango or fall ango (September through November). Concluding the week is a different schedule on Sunday, with most of the morning open to the public and a time-off period (called *hosan*) lasting from 2:00 P.M. Sunday to 2:00 P.M. Tuesday. These variances and others are discussed later in the chapter. The weekly schedule changes somewhat during the less intensive summer and winter training periods between angos. It may also differ in some details for a particular weekend or weeklong retreat.

As you imaginatively go through the different practices described below, bear in mind that they may vary slightly at other Zen institutions. For example, at Zen Mountain Monastery, kinhin (walking meditation) is always conducted between periods of zazen, but individuals can choose to remain seated in zazen instead of participating. At other places, everyone may be expected to do kinhin at such a time. Also, *oryo-ki* (the formal Zen process of eating) may be offered on more or fewer occasions at other Zen places than it is at Zen Mountain Monastery.

For now, however, let's begin a typical weekday on Mt. Tremper.

4:30 A.M.: Wake-up. BOOM! A cannonball shatters the living room wall. My grandfather's fake hair bursts into flames.

BOOM! A second cannonball. . . . No, it's a drum, the big drum way down in the zendo and, yes, a tiny bell coming closer and closer, ringing right outside the dorm room door, then moving away. The light in the dorm flips on.

Like nine other men around me, some of them bunked at my level in the room, the rest in lower bunks, I scringe and squirm from underneath a deep blue blanket. Scrounging into my clothes, I'm one of the first ones out into the hall and—*Yes!*—inside one of the two bathrooms on the floor. Then, sensing more and more sand-caked eyes focusing on the other side of the door, I'm out again as quickly as possible. I return to the dorm, grab my robe, and trot down three flights of stairs to the dining room for a cup of coffee and, just maybe, a few stretching exercises. I look at a clock for the first time that morning. It says I have eight minutes.

During my first stays at the monastery, I consistently slept with my glow-in-the-dark travel alarm clock mere inches from my face, tucked between the mattress and the bunk frame. My first night I even set it to wake me up early, so I'd be sure to get a bathroom right away and have time for coffee. The next morning, seconds after a few tinny beeps had sounded, I was told by the dorm monitor—my bunkmate—not to use it again (to my discredit, I hadn't thought much about its capacity to disturb others). When I went to bed thereafter, I would simply will myself to wake up early. Inevitably I'd fumble to check my clock several times during the night, and I'd always wind up crawling out of bed even sooner than I'd intended.

Then I learned a wonderful lesson. One sesshin week I inadvertently came to the monastery without my clock, the only timepiece I ever carry with me. I had no choice but to trust myself and the in-house system of drums and bells, as most other people seemed to do. That week I slept longer and more deeply than I ever had before. Each morning I woke up with the drum, and, despite occasional waiting for a bathroom, I always had time for coffee and, usually, a few stretches. Far more satisfying, however, was the greater peace and solidarity I felt having let go of my petty private agenda.

5:00 to 6:30 A.M.: Zazen/Teaching (Dokusan or Daisan). In fact, everyone is seated in the zendo, quiet and motionless, by 4:50 A.M., as directed on the posted schedule. When someone is absent, a behind-the-scenes search is conducted. Before zazen itself begins, the abbot ceremoniously makes the rounds of zabutons, weaving up one row and down the next with his hands in gassho. Each person returns the gassho as he passes. It's a mutual first greeting of the day as well as a kind of inspection, the abbot making sure everyone is present and ready for training. Afterward the formal signal for the first thirty-five-minute period of zazen is given: three bells, with a fifteen-second interval between rings.

For me, coming to wakefulness in the zendo, as the morning itself does, is wonderfully gratifying. Slowly and gently the space around me brightens with sunlight while, simultaneously, my mind clarifies and my attentiveness deepens.

I especially appreciate this experience because I'm not what is called a morning person. When I learned in high school biology the rule of "recapitulating phylogeny," whereby every animal repeats in its embryonic development each preceding species in its evolutionary history, I immediately recognized that the rule also applied to my waking pattern. Every morning I recapitulate phylogeny, beginning as a sluggish, one-cell paramecium and then continuing in slow progression to become a flatworm, frog, mouse, sloth, chimpanzee, and, finally, a human being.

Having this tendency, I find that getting a very early start on the day by sitting zazen helps me focus my mind—and my energy—in the best possible way. Somehow I'm more naturally able to resist distractions.

Now, on this spring morning in the monastery, the distractions include leftover dream stuff internally and, on the outside, steadily more visible knots in the pine flooring, escalating bird chatter, and because it's chilly enough, the intermittent *plink-plonk*ing of the heating ducts. All these potential disturbances seem like isolated phenomena registering on various background screens of my consciousness: the visual screen, the auditory screen, the tactile screen, and so on. I can turn my attention from them relatively easily at this time of day and concentrate more effectively on my *hara*, my breath, my koan.

Suddenly the voice of the abbot's attendant calls out, "The dokusan line is now open for students sitting on the inside row of the north side." It's another fleeting distraction for some, but for me, kneeling in that row, it's a rallying cry. Grabbing my seiza bench, I run for the dokusan line, other inside-northerners thudding around me as they do the same. Our urgency is a traditional part of the ritual: It demonstrates eagerness, gets things done swiftly, and establishes the order of dokusans—which, in some cases, can determine whether an individual has one at all. Quickly resettling ourselves in a line at the back of the zendo, we resume zazen.

Minutes pass, then the abbot, inside the dokusan room, rings his bell. Ahead of me, the abbot's attendant responds by striking a bell that's mounted next to the first person in line. That person then dashes through the zendo door into the hallway outside the dokusan room. I now move from second spot to the head of the line. The people in back of me remain motionless in zazen.

More minutes pass, then the abbot's bell rings again. I strike the line bell myself (the attendant does it only for the first person) and hurry through the zendo door, leaving my bench on the zendo side for later retrieval. With my hands in gassho I take position in front of the dokusan door. It opens.

The student who entered earlier stands just inside the room to the left, her hands also in gassho. I stand beside her facing the altar across the room and together we do a full bow. It consists of dropping gently to our knees, touching the floor with our foreheads, raising our hands—palms upward—several inches above the floor on either side of our head (to indicate the raising of buddha consciousness), returning to our knees, and finally standing and giving a short bow from the waist with our hands in gassho. She leaves the room, closing the door behind her.

I now sidestep a few paces and I do another full bow that ends with a standing bow. Then I step forward and kneel on a mat, where Daido sits facing me in zazen posture. He raises his eyes and looks into mine. I state my name and practice. Our dokusan begins.

What happens next is a form of face-to-face teaching. The student asks a question about life, death, Zen, Buddhism, or some other spiritual matter of personal concern, and the teacher responds with what Zen calls a "direct pointing" to the truth. The process, content, and meaning of this exchange are unique to each individual. For this reason, a student is expected not to discuss any of these matters with others. To do so would be to weaken or compromise the dokusan experience for both the student and his or her listeners.

I can reveal here that dokusan (or daisan—the same activity with either of the two other teachers at the monastery besides the abbot) is one of the biggest challenges I face in Zen practice. The formal protocol around it, coming in the midst of zazen, is a skillful way of separating it from everything else and ensuring that one approaches it as seriously as possible. At its heart, however, it's a singularly intimate, pure, and intensely alive mode of teaching and learning—so much so that I'm often terrified of it.

Sometimes the problem presents itself as not being able to think of a question to ask. Yes, the field of possible inquiry is infinite. True, my mind is constantly roiling with wonder, confusion, uncertainty, and overall cluelessness. Nevertheless, I sometimes can't develop any question on the spot that I regard as a sufficiently smart, clear, or important one, or one that puts me in a good enough—or bad enough—light. I know that this kind of "regard" in itself is the inappropriate stumbling block, but time and again I shove it out in front of me and down I go, at least as I wait for the teacher's summoning bell.

On other occasions I feel frustrated because I can't come up with an answer. For several years now I've been involved in koan study with Daido. This means that my first obligation in dokusan is to present my understanding of the particular koan I've been working on—not in any intellectual way but in a more direct manner, as befits the dokusan context. Again, my rational, regarding, and ever oppositional mind can start spasming, fighting as best it can to have the first and last words.

In either case, the root of the problem for me is that dokusan is not a place where I can use a civilized being's standard interpersonal tools— intelligence, charm, and manipulation—to express myself, engage the other party, or gain anything in return. Sometimes I do realize what a blessing this is, but other times I feel very naked, vulnerable, and upset about it.

Hojin acknowledges having had a comparable difficulty with dokusan during her early years at the monastery. She admits, "It took me a while to get used to the language of it, also the freedom of it. What kept coming up for me was fear. I really wanted to be free about it, but I had this need for approval. Eventually I began to like that the teacher was not going to give me anything, that it was not a matter of getting something from someone else."

For Gido, dokusan has always been the most compelling element of his life at the monastery. "It's what brings me to the zendo," he claims. "It's why I'm here. I struggle to have a good connection with the teacher as well as with other people, to go below the surface, to expose a deeper place. That's what happens in dokusan. It's undistracted by other things, and that's why I value it so much."

Troy has also loved dokusan from the beginning, but he is equally capable of dreading it. "Often I have the sense of what Daido's looking for," he claims, "but I know I'm not ready to go there. I don't yet trust myself. But then, dokusan calls me on that. It puts a fire underneath me. It keeps me on track."

Dokusan doesn't last long: sometimes only a few seconds, seldom more than a few minutes. After dokusan on this day, I return to my seat and resume sitting zazen. At the end of the period, the timekeeper (*jikido*) rings the bell twice. Everyone who wants to do kinhin then rises and, after a standing bow, turns to begin walking.

On each side of the zendo, a single, winding file of walkers, proceeding at a moderate pace, creates the identical pattern of movement around its rows of zabutons. Meanwhile, each individual doing kinhin applies the same undistracted mindfulness to walking that he or she has just been practicing in zazen.

After about ten minutes, the jikido claps wooden blocks to indicate the last round. Everyone continues walking until reaching his or her seat. The jikido then rings the bell to mark the end of kinhin. Everyone resumes sitting, this time facing the wall rather than the center of the zendo—and the people on the opposite side—as before. The rest of the zazen periods during the day will also be spent facing the wall until the last one, when everyone will once again turn toward the center.

Now three rings signal a second thirty-five-minute period of zazen and, for others, a chance to have dokusan. Midway through the sitting, in addition to an occasional exchange of bells between the abbot and the next dokusan student, I start hearing the *thwack . . . thwack* of the *kyosaku,* a flattened stick about a yard long that one of the monitors uses to strike acupressure points on a sitter's two shoulders. The purpose of this somewhat strange and commonly misunderstood act is to help alleviate a sitter's soreness or fatigue, not to administer discipline or to surprise a sleeping student into wakefulness.

The monitor never hits you with the kyosaku unless you give your permission. As you sit, you eventually hear or see (out of your eye corners) the monitor slowly advancing down the line toward your zabuton. If you want the kyosaku, you wait until the monitor is almost in front of you and then you put your hands in gassho, the palms-together expression of reverence. The monitor faces you, the two of you bow to each other, and you lean forward, moving your head one way and then the other so that the monitor can hit each shoulder. The sound can be shockingly loud because of the stick's reverberant design, but the blows themselves are stimulating rather than painful. After they're given, the two of you bow to each other again. The monitor moves on, and you return to zazen.

This zazen period doesn't end with kinhin. Instead, a different bell is rung and everyone, still sitting, gasshos and joins in chanting the traditional "Verse of the Kesa":

> *Vast is the robe of liberation,*
> *A formless field of benefaction.*
> *I wear the Tathagata's [the Buddha's] teachings,*
> *Saving all sentient beings.*

The "Verse of the Kesa" is chanted three times. At the beginning of the second chanting, everyone who has a kesa (certain monastics) or a rakasu (other monastics and laypeople) takes the folded garment from its cover, previously laid on the zabuton, and places it, still folded, on top of his or her head. Thus one begins to "wear the Tathagata's teachings" for that day.

I am always moved by this unusual and special moment. With my rakasu balanced above me, I sense a vibrant connection with countless others in time and space: from the people in the zendo both now and before to all followers of the Buddhist way both now and before. It is as if my rakasu, made up of patches, were itself one tiny fragment in the vastness of the Buddha's robe. By the beginning of the third chant, when I actually put on my rakasu, that feeling of connection has at last expanded to include all sentient beings—not just in the here and now but everywhere in the past, present, and future.

6:30 to 6:50 A.M.: Morning Service. After the "Verse of the Kesa," the densho (big bell) hanging in back of the zendo is struck, and everyone prepares for morning service. Some individuals have specific positions to take up. The others, like myself, tidy the zabutons, making sure each one has a zafu in the lower outside corner, and then stand in the center of any free zabuton, so that no gaps exist in the rows facing each other across the zendo.

Between the two sets of rows, and directly in front of the altar, is a carpeted area called the *rioban*. Its south side is reserved for certain designated monastics, including the *ino* (chant leader); the north side, for certain designated laypeople. A mat in the middle of the rioban marks the bowing place of the officiant, who may be a teacher, a senior monastic, or a senior layperson.

Now, as the students in the rows and the designated individuals on the rioban wait for the officiant, everything is momentarily still but infused with vigilance.

From the beginning of dawn zazen through morning service, I sometimes feel as if I were one in a crew of people sailing across the ocean on a big wooden ship. The zendo's wooden floors and wall borders, the discipline required of both individuals and the group, and the boat-shaped layout of sitting and standing positions all help to reinforce the illusion.

So do the sounds of the bells and clappers that punctuate different parts of the schedule. When I first visited here, I didn't know that this kind of signaling system was a centuries-old tradition in Zen monasteries. I figured it was a legacy of Daido's navy years that was unique to this place. It was an understandable assumption: The system does serve exactly the same functions in Zen monasteries and on navy ships: namely, letting everyone know the time of day, the action to take, and/or the approximate location of a certain person (or thing) in motion.

The zendo can also seem like a ship to me because of a major symbol in Buddhism that relates both to zazen and to Zen practice in general—the image of "crossing the water" from everyday consciousness to the "far shore" of enlightenment. It occurs, for example, in the *Heart Sutra,* chanted during each morning service here and in virtually every other Mahayana Buddhist institution around the world: *"Gate, gate, paragate"* or, in some translations, "Further, further, to the farthest [shore]" (see p. 174).

Buddhism's birthplace in India is riddled with streams and rivers that flood during monsoon season, so it's small wonder that many Buddhist concepts relate to water. The religion itself is divided into three different schools called *yanas* (literally, "ferries") Zen being one sect of the Mahayana ("great ferry") vehicle. Even the basic doctrines pertaining to the impermanence of all things and the oneness of form and

Geoffrey Shugen Arnold, Sensei (left), officiates at the altar during a service. He is attended by Jinzan, a resident lay student.

emptiness may have evolved from the extraordinarily creative and destructive presence of water in the Ganges River plains and the Bay of Bengal coastlands. As for me, while I'm waiting for morning service to start, my mind can easily stray toward imagining that we've all mustered on deck during a journey across a sea that is sometimes smooth, sometimes turbulent.

Morning service begins when the officiant enters from the back of the zendo: in this case, Shugen Sensei, one of the teachers. His progress to the altar is punctuated by an attendant's bell communicating with the bell of the main instrumentalist (*doan*), who is seated to the right of the altar.

After Shugen has gone to the altar and returned to the mat in the center of the rioban, he leads everyone present in three full bows toward the altar's image of the Buddha. As usual, bells provide timing guidance for those who can't see the officiant out of the corners of their eyes.

During the service, everyone present chants two sutras, beginning with the *Heart Sutra*. Meanwhile Shugen, assisted by his attendants, performs various rituals at the altar. The service ends with three full bows, but the people in the side rows remain standing as first Shugen and then the people on the rioban process out of the zendo. After a standing bow to each other, everyone remaining in the zendo smooths out his or her zabuton, restores the cushion to the center of it, and bows in a gesture of leave-taking.

7:00 to 8:00 A.M.: Art Practice/Body Practice. Following a break for changing out of robes and using the bathroom, everyone gathers downstairs in the dining hall to begin an hour of art practice. Every other day, the same hour is devoted instead to body practice: yoga, running, walking, or whatever else one has signed up to do.

For temporary or permanent residents at the monastery during ango—as well as ango participants at home—art practice involves creating a work that relates to the particular *Shobogenzo* section under study. You can choose among various media in the visual, musical, or performing arts. Many prefer a traditional Zen art form like haiku, brush painting, or shakuhachi, since it feeds so directly into Zen training. Others gravitate toward art forms that are more familiar in the West, like photography, free verse, sculpture, or computer art. Whatever project you decide to do, it needs to be checked out in advance with the training office to make sure it's appropriate.

Most of the time I choose storytelling for art practice. I occasionally opt for another medium just to experiment with something new. Once I even designed a totem pole featuring Buddhist icons. Storytelling, however, has always brought me the most growth, the keenest insights, the greatest range of pains and pleasures.

As a person who tells stories professionally, I find that the ango art project provides me with a unique context in which to confront my craft with beginner's mind and take risks I might not otherwise allow myself. Jimon alludes to this opportunity for creative breakthrough in her interview quoted earlier (see chapter 3). The challenge is to drop the showy business of any artistic skills you've acquired so that the work you produce issues more authentically out of your experience. Rough and raw though the product may appear, the process can be profoundly emancipating and illuminating.

Today, after introductory remarks by the art practice supervisors, I go off into the woods beyond the big meadow. When I'm reasonably sure I'm alone and out of earshot, I begin spinning a story out loud—in this case one from my personal life—that reflects my understanding of the section. The trees, the rocks, and an unknown number of unseen creatures are my listeners. They're not without their critical impact. Sometimes I'm ashamed of the artificial things I utter in their natural presence. But I continue, striving to externalize what my mind and heart want to communicate, until it begins to sound—and feel—right.

I take this form of verbalization all the more seriously because it occurs during a period of official silence. Each day the monastery's precaution against speaking (except for chanting, dokusan/daisan, work instructions, or emergencies) lasts from evening zazen through caretaking in the morning, which, at the moment, is another hour and a half away. My storytelling, like the singing that some others are doing for their art project, is a special exemption from the rule.

8:00 to 8:30 A.M.: Oryoki Formal Breakfast. Returning from the woods to the dining hall, I join the rest of the sangha in assembling for breakfast. First I pick up my mess kit (to use a military metaphor) from the place where I laid it neatly among the others after the last time. The cantaloupe-sized bundle consists of three black plastic nesting bowls, two chopsticks, a wooden spoon, a small rubber spatula, a gray napkin, and a wiping cloth, all of which are wrapped up tidily in a gray cloth with a topknot resembling a lotus blossom. Holding it in both hands just above eye level, I walk to the table and stand before an open seat. When everyone else has done the same, we bow to each other, set our bundles on the table in front of us, sit down on the long bench, and begin the formal oryoki (literally, "just enough") breakfast.

Cued by the ino's clappers, we chant a special liturgy as we unfold the top-knotted cloth, lay it out as a place mat, and arrange our bowls and utensils on top of it in the prescribed pattern. Other cues signal the passing of large bowls or pitchers of food and drink from one chanting diner to the next. Typical provisions include hot cereal, fruit, juice, and assorted breads. As each bowl or pitcher comes to me, I return the passer's bow and take "just enough" to satisfy my hunger: All food must be eaten in a limited amount of time and there are no second portions. I then pass the bowl or pitcher to the next person, bowing as I do.

Eating begins for the entire group when the serving process is over. During this period, as before, I keep my eyes lowered. I also try to stay as quiet and composed as I can—for example, by not making noise with my spoon against the bowl and not wiggling around as I sit.

The ino signals when it's time for us to stop eating and start cleaning. My initial act, aside from wolfing down any remaining food, is to scrape each bowl with the spatula and lick the spatula clean of food particles. Then hot water (actually a light tea) is passed around. I take just enough into my biggest bowl for the washing. Rubbing the inside of this water-filled bowl with the spatula, I dislodge lingering food residue into the water, pour the water into the next bowl, and repeat the process. I dry each bowl—and the utensils that I wash in the second one— with the wiping cloth.

Now comes the wrap-up. I drink the cleaning water from the last bowl, leaving a small amount to offer "hungry ghosts" (beings who symbolize constant hunger and suffering; see glossary, "Six worlds"). During another round of chanting, an urn is passed from person to person, and I pour my offering into this urn. Then I rebundle my bowls and utensils into the place mat cloth and fold the four corners on top to look like a lotus blossom.

Finally, we all rise, by cue, to a standing position with our bundles again held slightly above eye level. After bowing right, left, and forward, we file over to the place where we neatly lay our bundles in readiness for the next breakfast.

I describe oryoki in such detail for a reason: The intricacy of the ritual in itself requires an especially thorough and rewarding application of mindfulness. On an obvious level, you learn to value food, the process of eating, and the pleasure of entering into that process in a calm and graceful manner. On a subtler level, you develop a better understanding of what is "just enough" or "the right amount" in your life: not only in terms of nourishment or comfort but also in terms of movement, energy, and concentration.

Jimon once spoke about the latter issue in a talk during Sunday service. "If our oryoki practice doesn't ever leave breakfast," she cautioned, "we're really missing an incredible teaching, an incredible opportunity to study ourselves."

Besides revealing graphically to Jimon her habit of taking more food than she needed, oryoki taught her that she tended to approach life in general with too much exertion. "I used to do oryoki with very little attention to its inner harmony," she confided in her talk. "When I would hold my bowls, I would grip them as if I were holding a twenty-pound dumbbell. I would scrape my bowls clean and do it as if I were trying to remove tar. When I realized I was doing this, it seemed consistent with the way I'd always done everything—overkill, with extremely intense energy. Living one's life this way can be pretty exhausting. Not only is it exhausting, it's unnecessary and most likely out of harmony with the action itself." (Here and above, as reprinted in "Giving Means Nongreed," *Mountain Record*, spring 1993, pp. 34–39)

For others, oryoki's teachings are slightly different. I sometimes catch myself being too lax or inattentive, forgetting to follow a certain procedural step because I've let my mind wander, even if only off to the side to relish the sheer beauty of the ceremony.

In Robert's case, oryoki taught him to be less obstinately fussy about what he ate—a lesson that he admits he could also apply to other experiences in life. "The first day the oatmeal came around," he recalls, "I took a spoonful because I felt I had to put something in the first bowl. I'm one of those people who have always hated oatmeal without ever trying it out. That first bite was fine—no big deal, but not disgusting. Three days later, I was up to three spoonfuls and I sort of liked it. It's amazing what a kick it is to get beyond a little prejudice like that."

9:00 to 10:00 A.M.: Caretaking Practice. After oryoki there is a half-hour break in the schedule, during which the people on breakfast crew (others are on lunch or supper crew) clean the cooking dishes and kitchen. Shortly before the break is over, someone strikes an extended pattern on the han—the highly resonant wooden board in the zendo hallway—to summon everyone inside the main building to the buddha hall for caretaking practice.

The buddha hall, located on the other side of the hallway from the zendo, is a one-story room with about a third of the zendo's floor space. It, too, has an altar facing a central area used for ceremonial purposes. People gathering in the room, either for certain forms of instruction or for caretaking assignments, form rows on either side of this area. They also take off their shoes before entering the room, just as they do before entering the zendo, and store them temporarily in the same wooden racks along the hallway wall.

I enter the buddha hall and, seeing more space on the other side of the room, walk over to it, stopping for a short, standing bow as I pass in front the altar. Students are expected to make the same gesture of respect toward the zendo altar as they cross the zendo or pass through the zendo hallway. After joining a row, I stand with my hands clasped at my waist and my eyes lowered, waiting for the caretaking ceremony to begin.

Life at the monastery brings many moments of attentive waiting. At first I found them aggravating. I'd quickly start squirming mentally and physically, which only made time seem to drag along even more slowly. Gradually, over the weeks, months, and years, I have learned to value these (usually) brief occasions more and more. They are humbling to me in the best possible way, gently training me to be patient and ever ready for whatever occurs. They also serve as unexpected openings in the day, when my mind can clear itself as it does in zazen and get another small taste of freedom. I've come to consider this kind of active stillness as a more expansive form of listening—one that doesn't focus narrowly on specific sounds.

A drumbeat gives the cue. Jimon, the work leader, advances to the altar and, assisted by the altar usher and the jikido, offers incense before the statue of Manjushri, bodhisattva of wisdom. Everyone then joins in chanting the work gatha (a verse from the *Heart Sutra*). Afterward Jimon reads aloud the work assignments from a prepared sheet.

For the most part, the tasks involve routine, fairly simple maintenance tasks: for example, weeding the garden, cleaning the bathrooms, stacking firewood, washing the four monastery cars, peeling potatoes, preparing the latest copies of *Mountain Record* for mailing, sanding newly built seiza benches in the woodshop, polishing the brass items on all the main building altars. Assignments are rotated daily, so that each of us—monk or lay student, long-term resident or weeklong retreatant—gets to experience a range of different, unanticipated chores.

The point of the caretaking period in the schedule is to engage all of us who are present at the monastery in helping it to function on the most basic level. Through this effort, we can not only express our gratitude to the monastery in a very personal way but also, over time, educate ourselves about the many things that go on here and that need tending on a regular basis.

Sometimes we get assignments that match our skills, which, for residents and retreatants alike, are recorded in the work leader's files. For example, I'm often asked to copyedit manuscripts or to transcribe correspondence to prisoners that Shugen has dictated (Zen Mountain Monastery has a vigorous prison outreach program, including sponsorship of an affiliate group, the Lotus Flower Sangha, at the Green Haven Correctional Facility in nearby Poughkeepsie, New York).

Other times we are challenged to take on tasks that do not fit our skills profile. For me, those jobs have included helping to put up drywall, lay stone floor tiles, and dig irrigation trenches.

In addition to educating us about specific chores, caretaking provides a special, self-contained chance to test and refine our approach to work in general. It presents each of us with questions that are well worth answering on the spot.

- What self-limiting attitudes or prejudices do I have about doing certain things?
- How much of myself do I give to what I am doing?
- What happens when I hold back from it? When I devote all my attention and energy to it?

The simplicity, variety, and brevity of the caretaking tasks—relative to the more skilled and longer-term labors undertaken during each day's work practice periods—make it somewhat easier to maintain a beginner's mind and a whole-hearted concentration as we do them.

It's also helpful that caretaking occurs while the silence precaution is still in effect. Even though I occasionally need to talk with someone during caretaking in order to do my job, and even though I'm expected to keep conversation to a minimum during the work practice periods later in the day, I notice that the atmosphere during caretaking has an especially deep quietness. For me, this inspires a correspondingly greater degree of inner stillness that enables me to become more absorbed in what I'm doing.

As already mentioned (see chapter 2), Sara claims to have had an especially intense and gratifying caretaking experience the morning she picked strawberries in the garden. She adds, however, that it occurred the second morning she was there and that she didn't even show up for caretaking practice the first morning. "I was totally lame about it," she confesses. "At other places I've been, mostly New Age–type places, they use the word *caretaking* to mean 'taking care of yourself.' So, when I saw this period on the [monastery] schedule, I assumed it was a time to be private, you know, to reflect, to wash out some clothes, whatever. It isn't as if you get much time for that here! Five minutes before the period ended, they finally found me sitting by the stream, spacing out."

The next day Sara was understandably determined to participate in caretaking practice as well as she possibly could, and the results for her were especially fulfilling. "That second time," she says, "I had the strange feeling that I was, once again, taking care of myself, but this time in a far more powerful way. I wasn't indulging myself, like before, when I was trying to get away from it all and not do much of anything. Instead, I was letting myself live through what I was doing."

10:00 A.M. 12:00 noon: Work Practice/Retreat Sessions. After caretaking comes work practice or, if you're attending a retreat, the first retreat session of the day, which the leader organizes as he or she sees fit. In my case, it's work practice.

Jimon again announces the assignments, this time in the dining hall. They are often more complex than the caretaking ones. For monastics and long-term residents, they may be ongoing jobs pursued during every work practice period for months or even years: for example, serving as head cook, bookkeeper, or editor of the *Mountain Record*. For short-term residents and retreatants, they're usually more isolated projects that last anywhere from one period to a full week of periods: for example, transplanting evergreens, sewing zabutons, designing a computer layout, building new shelving, or running errands to local stores and farms.

12:00 to 12:30 P.M.: Lunch; 1:30 to 5:00 P.M.: Work Practice/Retreat Sessions. At noon Gido, the cook, rings the bell hanging outside the kitchen door. Like everyone else, I've had about fifteen minutes to clean up and catch my breath after work practice, and now I join the mob scurrying into the dining hall for lunch. The mob quickly resolves itself into a hushed assembly of proper Zen students, each of us standing—once again—perfectly still with hands clasped at the waist and eyes lowered.

Our focal point, at least from the corners of our eyes, is the dining room altar below the bell. There Gido offers food from the meal and incense before the statue of Fudo, a godly figure (carried over from Hinduism to Buddhism) who symbolizes protection from fire. Gido then unrolls a mat at the foot of the altar cabinet and does three full bows, while everyone else in the room accompanies them with standing bows. The ino then cues the meal gatha, and all of us join in this chant expressing our gratitude to the universe for the food and our intention to reciprocate by following the buddha way:

> First, seventy-two labors brought us this food; we should
> know how it comes to us.

> *Second, as we receive this offering, we should consider*
> *whether our virtue and practice deserve it.*
> *Third, as we desire the natural order of mind to be free from*
> *clinging, we must be free from greed.*
> *Fourth, to support our life we take this food.*
> *Fifth, to attain our way we take this food.*
> *First, this food is for the three treasures.*
> *Second, it is for our teachers, parents, nation, and all sen-*
> *tient beings.*
> *Third, it is for all beings in the six worlds.*
> *Thus, we eat this food with everyone.*
> *We eat to stop all evil, to practice good, to save all sentient*
> *beings, and to accomplish our buddha way.*

The silence precaution is lifted until evening zazen. Social chattering arises and prevails, both in the line to fill our plates at the serving tables and among the large eating tables, now spread out into different areas of the dining room. The meal itself is the most substantial of the day—a vegetarian main course, rice, salad, and, as always, plenty of bread, butter, margarine, peanut butter, jelly, coffee, and assorted teas and powdered drinks. Altogether, the atmosphere is very relaxed and even festive, compared with the quiet, intense nature of the rest of the day.

When the weather is warm, it's nice to eat lunch (or, later, supper) outside on the semicircular steps or at the picnic tables beyond them. For many people, especially those who live in the main building and have caretaking and work practice indoors, it may be the single best opportunity during the day to enjoy the natural beauty surrounding the monastery.

The fact that there isn't much time during the day to spend outdoors has always struck me as one of the biggest ironies of life at the monastery. Zen puts a high value on the teachings of nature, and the local land, water, plants, animals, and sky are remarkably beautiful, and yet the

The grounds of most Zen monasteries feature many different kinds of places to sit, walk, exercise, lie down, or otherwise relax. Here a retreatant sits on the stone wall. In the foreground is a pole raised by visiting Japanese monks to celebrate Daido's 1989 installation as abbot.

training takes place mostly indoors. I have to remind myself that this training helps make the outdoors much more vital and inspirational to me when I *do* get to be there.

This lunch period, for instance, as I lie down on the lawn after eating, the freshly green, translucent grass fills my senses—including my mind, which, according to Buddhism, is only another sense. It's a timeless experience, so how can I even begin to think of it in terms of time—short or long?

Gido tells me that he also benefits a great deal from the nature surrounding the monastery, even though he doesn't get to see it much. "I'm lucky to live in a cabin," he says, "so I'm outdoors going back and forth to the main building. Still, there's no time during the week to explore it. My first month here, I was really angry about the running around we have to do, and the pressure there is to get to places in a short amount of time. I didn't like having to dash down the muddy hillside in my robes. Now I understand it better as part of the level of dedication here, and I don't get the same kind of anger. I may not have any time to roam around outdoors, but I appreciate it. I'm grateful for it. Its presence affects everything here."

Lunch is followed by roughly an hour of free time, assuming you aren't on lunch crew. I'm not, and after lying in the grass for a while, I take a shower. It's not the time of day I normally shower at home, but here you have to grab whatever chance you have. Showering is not permitted before dawn zazen or after evening zazen, when there's a heavy demand for the bathrooms, so it's only really feasible after lunch or supper. Because I'm on supper crew, the after-lunch period is better: More time means more chance that a bathroom will become available.

Daily life at the monastery can be full of such private calculations. I have to guard against too much preplanning because it feeds expectations and desires—the very entities Buddhism warns against as primary sources of suffering. What if I don't get a shower today? Will that depress me? What if I do get a shower, but it doesn't refresh me as much as I thought it would? Will that discourage me?

There's another, equally important reason for me not to become caught up in strategizing every minute of the day so that it's as good or as painless as it can be. I may wind up coasting through the day on my plans and miss really participating in it moment by moment as it evolves. I've learned from experience that this latter kind of engagement is the one that truly matters, the only one that can help me realize more about myself and the world around me.

Anyway, it's no crime to want to shower at some point during the day, and I manage to do it after lunch. When I finish, it's time to report to the dining hall with every other nonretreatant for the second period of work practice. Meanwhile, the retreatants have their second daily session with their instructor, which proceeds, as does the morning session, according to the instructor's directions.

5:00 to 6:00 P.M.: Zazen and Evening Service; 6:00 to 6:30 P.M.: Light Supper. By 5:00 P.M. we have all finished work practice or the second retreat session, tidied up, and taken our seats in the zendo. The jikido rings the bell, and we begin zazen.

This period of zazen—even though it consists of only one thirty-five-minute sitting—tends to be rough for me. I'm tired from the afternoon, plus it's the time of day at home when I like to knock off work and do something mindless until dinner. Now I am recalled to pure mindfulness, and it's hard. Thoughts and feelings come back from the day to roost, cluck, and crow. One by one I acknowledge them and send them on their way, but they're bent on homing, and more than the usual number fly back again and again.

The same thing may be occurring in other people's minds and translating into slumpy posture or collapsed mudras, for all of a sudden a monitor at the back of the zendo shouts, "WAKE UP! This is your life! Do not sleep through it! If the zendo were in flames, you would be wide awake! Sit with a fire on your head!" The monitor's words ring in *my* head like a firehouse alarm, as they were intended to do. The shock of them turns instantly into gratitude. I sit with new energy and much better concentration.

The densho is rung at the end of the sitting, and evening service begins. It's shorter than morning service and involves a different chant but follows approximately the same format. At its conclusion, we straighten the zabuton we're standing on, plump the zafu, place it in the center of the zabuton, bow to it, and leave the zendo, bowing toward the altar as we pass the threshold into the hallway (something we're expected to do whenever we cross that threshold, coming or going). We then put on our shoes and wend our way to the dining hall for supper, which is about five minutes away.

Once again Gido rings the bell above the dining room altar, at which point we all stand with our hands clasped at the waist. He then makes an offering before Fudo of incense and some of the food he's prepared. For this lightest meal of the day—usually soup, salad, and bread—there is no chanting: We simply do three standing bows to accompany Gido's full bows.

Like lunch, supper offers an opportunity to socialize, debate, or confer on the day's business, if you're so inclined and if you have the time. I get into a half-serious, half-joking discussion about the duration of a *kalpa*, a Sanskrit term used in Buddhism to represent, among other things, the incredibly long period of time that passes between earthly appearances of a great buddha.

Various Buddhist texts attempt to define the infinite length of a kalpa by creating different metaphorical scenarios. For example, one source describes a kalpa as the time it would take for an eagle to wear away an entire mountain if it merely brushed the top of it with its wing once a century. Another asks the reader to imagine that a one-holed wooden yoke floats in the ocean and a one-eyed turtle rises somewhere on the ocean's surface once a century: A kalpa represents how long it would be until the turtle happened to rise through the yoke's hole. Our discussion at the dining hall table supplements these illustrations with ones involving space travel and golf balls in the Grand Canyon.

Fortunately or unfortunately, I have only twenty minutes to participate in the discussion. As a member of supper crew, I report to the kitchen at 6:30. The crew leader assigns me to the dish room. I stand in front of a plastic dishpan of soapy water. Diners pass by, leaving their plates, glasses, and silverware for me to prewash and load into racks that I eventually run through the institutional dishwasher behind me. People who turn in their dishes before the crew is on duty, or who use cups or glasses at other times of the day, are expected to do the prewashing and racking themselves.

As I work with the dishes, others are putting away leftover food, washing and drying pots and pans at the large kitchen sink, taking out the compost and trash, wiping the dining room tables, making new coffee, and mopping the floor. We operate in rather speedy precision: The sooner we get the job done well, the more free time we'll have before evening zazen. Everyone works, changing tasks if necessary, until the kitchen, dish room, and dining hall are clean and ready for the next meal. At that time, the crew leader gasshos to each of us, and we disperse.

I take a cup of coffee to the semicircular steps outside the dining room's east doors. The benches in the recessed doorway are filled with smokers, this being the unofficially designated smoking area, with its own, floor-standing wooden ashtray looking like a small baptismal font. I sprawl across the steps among others doing the same. The declining sun gilds everything around us. In the beauty of the light, the talk is gentle, low, and interlaced with many moments of silent enjoyment.

Diane especially likes this hour (a full one for those not on supper crew). "I look forward to it as a time to reflect on everything that has happened during the day," she says. "For me, it's the prelude to evening zazen and then sleep—a winding down of things. I like to roam around the grounds, stretch my legs, practice a little of the focus I put into the rest of things, but now at my own pace and for my own purposes. The deer are out foraging then, and I almost always see a few, sometimes even right out in the meadow, in plain sight of anyone on the steps. I love feeling the kinship I do with them, at least at that hour. We are all slowly concluding our day of living on the mountain."

7:30 to 9:00 P.M.: Zazen/Teaching (Dokusan or Daisan); 9:30 P.M.: Lights Out. At 7:20 the jikido starts pounding the han to summon everyone to zazen: two thirty-five-minute sittings, during which dokusan or daisan is usually announced. Wednesday evenings are open to nonresidents, both students and individuals who simply want to visit the monastery. Because this is Wednesday, about a dozen extra people are seated on zafus, benches, and chairs, mostly nonresident students hoping to get face-to-face teaching. Others who are here for the first time are going into the buddha hall for beginning instruction during the first period of zazen. The jikido rings the bell three times and zazen begins.

Many people, including myself, sometimes experience muscular discomfort during zazen, which may or may not be the kind that a kyosaku can help alleviate. It mostly depends on how tired we are, how accustomed we've become to the posture we're using, and our basic physical constitutions. Another contributing factor, however, is attitude.

For me, evening zazen can be physically tough because I am often tired and I have a herniated disk in my back. Over the years, however, I've learned to accept whatever pain I feel as just another sensation. It's not bad or wrong in itself, doesn't threaten my life, and won't get better if I wiggle around. As long as I stay focused on my zazen practice, the pain is okay for the time being and occasionally vanishes altogether. Whenever I start dwelling on the pain, it escalates dramatically.

Robert also speaks of this phenomenon. "The very first time I sat zazen, my legs ached as they never had before," he tells me. "It seemed excruciating to me, but I understand now that *excruciating* was only the word I was yelling in my head. Actually, it was just something different. Panic can set in whenever you're encountering something strange, particularly something physically uncomfortable. Well, I kept gutting it out that first day. I was too vain to switch to a bench or chair, even though I'd been told it was perfectly all right to do that. When I brought up this pain to one of the monks, she said it sounded as if I were enduring the pain instead of being one with it, just giving myself up to it. Well, I took her advice the next time I sat zazen, and, what do you know, it worked!"

At the end of the first sitting period this evening, the bell rings twice, and I rise to do kinhin with most of the others. A few remain sitting in zazen throughout kinhin. It's always an option, but I rarely take it. One reason is, frankly, soreness. After thirty-five minutes my weak back typically cries out for exercise to a degree that's especially distracting. Another is that I'm very drawn to walking meditation. I find that putting all my concentration into moving forward physically, step by step, helps extend and reinforce the work I've done on my seiza bench, clearing my mind of some of the motes still stirring within it and bringing it more into harmony with my body.

Aside from clasping my hands at my waist, I walk normally at a moderate pace, focusing on the act itself but also being sensitive to the movements of the person in front of me and the pattern I'm following around and around the rows of zabutons on my side of the zendo. Ex–track runner that I am, I feel as if I'm training myself to proceed through life in the way I was meant to do, as naturally and aware as possible.

Of course, when I realize I'm dwelling on that feeling, I acknowledge it and, quite often, manage to let it go. I do the same when less germane stuff arises, such as my hunger for a massage, the fantasy that

I'm a holy man, or the song lyrics "Heigh Ho! Heigh Ho! It's Off to Work We Go!"

Kinhin ends and we sit down for the day's last period of zazen. We've turned our zafus, benches, or chairs around so that the rows on either side of the zendo face each other, just as they did during the day's first period of zazen. It's like coming back together after sixteen-plus hours of mindful living in the same environment. Joining us are the first-timers who have received beginning instruction and are now ready to put what they've learned into practice.

The bell rings and we resume zazen. Before long I hear the sound of a car slowly moving down the gravel road toward the main building and stopping outside the kitchen door, right below the zendo's north-side windows. The car door opens and shuts.

The abbot's attendant, sitting with the monitors at the back of the zendo, instantly rises and announces, "The dokusan line is open to all nonresident students who have not had dokusan in two weeks." I overhear a quick stampede to the line and register the thought that at least some of the outside students will get face-to-face teaching tonight.

I return to zazen. A few minutes later, the abbot rings his bell in the dokusan room, and the attendant rings in response on behalf of the first student in the dokusan line. A more direct back-and-forth signaling between abbot and upcoming student occurs every now and then during the rest of the sitting.

Zazen ends around 8:50 P.M. with a cue to remain sitting, put our hands in gassho, and chant the four bodhisattva vows three times:

> *Sentient beings are numberless; I vow to save them.*
> *Desires are inexhaustible; I vow to put an end to them.*
> *The dharmas are boundless; I vow to master them.*
> *The buddha way is unattainable; I vow to attain it.*

After the four bodhisattva vows, the jikido plays a pattern on the drum, densho, and han that marks the time of day. Then, as the rest of us listen with our hands in gassho, the ino chants the evening gatha:

> *Let me respectfully remind you,*
> *life and death are of supreme importance.*
> *Time swiftly passes by and opportunity is lost.*
> *Each of us should strive to awaken.*
> *Awaken. Take heed.*
> *Do not squander your life.*

The jikido does three runs on the han, and everyone rises. The abbot, who has already entered the zendo, is standing before the mat on the rioban. He leads us in doing three full bows toward the Buddha statue on the altar.

After Daido and then Shugen walk out of the zendo, the usual procedure is for us to bow to each other (that is, toward the center of the zendo), smooth out our zabuton, place a plumped-up zafu in the center, leave the zendo, and silently prepare for lights out at 9:30 P.M.. However, things are different on Wednesday evenings, thanks to the presence of visitors. Before it's time for us to leave the zendo, one of the monitors announces that the normal silence precaution is lifted until 9:30 so that we can talk with each other in the dining room. What's more, refreshments are being provided!

Whatever homemade item is served—cookies, cake, brownies, cobbler, pudding, or baklava—it's a welcome treat in the dessertless week for most of us residents. We pounce. We also pump visitors for information about what's happening in the outside world. In general, we like being cut off from the media at the monastery and, as a result, from the direct intrusion of current events into our lives. Nevertheless, a small dose of news on Wednesday night is in keeping with the refreshments: just enough worldly matter to keep us from feeling deprived.

At about 9:25 the lights in the dining room flicker. The jikido, who needs to close up the monastery for the night before getting to sleep herself, is sending a subtle message. A few minutes later, the visitors have left and the residents have gone to their beds. After lights out, indicated in the main building by the jikido's walking through the hallways ringing a bell, all residents are expected to stay in bed sleeping, unless they choose to sit zazen for a while in the zendo, where the lights burn dimly all night long.

Sunday, Hosan, and Sesshin

On Sunday we can sleep until 6:15 A.M. When we arise, the silence precaution is not in effect, and we chat through a hearty, informal breakfast that is served in the dining room at 6:45. From 7:45 to 8:45 we do caretaking practice, and then hurry to get ready for the 9:00 morning program open to the public. It includes a morning service, two sessions of zazen (for newcomers, beginning instruction during the first one), and a talk by Daido, Myotai, Shugen, or a senior monastic or lay student.

Afterward, around noon, everyone present—visitor or resident—gathers for a community lunch in the dining room. It always consists of pasta, two sauces (meat and vegetarian), salad, breads, and, for the one time in the week, dessert. The menu has as much to do with economic and self-serve practicality as it does with Daido's Italian background. A half hour into the lunch period, the monastery store opens for business at the back of the dining hall, selling practice-related books, tapes (including that morning's talk), art objects, and merchandise.

At 2:00 P.M. the monastery is again closed to visitors, and the residents have a two-day time-off period called hosan. They can use it to take care of their laundry as well as other personal business and/or to make trips into Phoenicia (five miles), Woodstock (ten miles), or even New York City (one hundred miles). For some, it's a chance to reinoculate themselves with fast food, chocolate, gourmet coffee, a movie . . . the list goes on! Others spend the time more meditatively, assimilating what they've experienced during the training week and maintaining a personal schedule that's somewhat similar in tone. Whether you're in one group or the other often depends on the week you've just lived through.

Hosan ends at 2:00 P.M. Tuesday when everyone reports for work practice in the dining hall. The rest of Tuesday proceeds as a normal weekday does.

Sesshin, which is open to the public via preregistration, takes place the third full week of each month. It begins at 5:00 P.M. Monday and lasts through Sunday morning. Essentially, each full day from Tuesday through Saturday features more than twice as much zazen—a total of seven hours per day in separate, thirty-five-minute sessions—punctuated by several opportunities for face-to-face teaching. Throughout this time span, the silence precaution remains in effect, except for teaching encounters and essential work practice exchanges. In addition to not talking with each other, it means not making or receiving telephone calls. Along with it are precautions against making eye contact, reading, or writing—all activities that can distract the mind from its focus on zazen.

Each sesshin day during ango seasons (nonango sesshins are slightly less intense), participants get up a half hour earlier than the normal schedule to allow for three periods of zazen before morning service. Then comes oryoki breakfast, even more formal this week than others during the month because it's eaten while seated on a zabuton in the zendo. It starts with heavy drumming and an impressive offertory ceremony involving the cook and head server. This beginning never fails to stir me even though my downcast eyes see it only peripherally. The food items are brought in separately by waiters fulfilling service positions. Each time, the exchange between server and seated diner is a precisely orchestrated one involving bowing and hand signaling to indicate portion size.

After breakfast and a brief period for changing clothes and resting (during which the servers eat oryoki style in the dining hall), everyone takes part in caretaking. Next are three more sitting periods, a noon serv-ice, and a formal oryoki lunch, also in the zendo. Lunch is followed by a one-hour rest period, two more sitting periods, a roughly forty-minute talk (by Daido, Shugen, Myotai, or a senior monastic or lay stu-dent), another sitting period, and evening service. There's a break at 6:00 P.M. for a self-serve supper downstairs, and then three more sitting peri-ods before lights out at 9:30.

Sunday morning begins at the same, early time during sesshin week. It features a single zazen session followed by an open *sosan,* an hour-long sitting period during which participants break silence as they are moved, Quaker-style, to share what the week was like for them. At the end of open sosan, various short, ceremonial events wind up the week and lift all precautions, although sesshin technically extends through the rest of the morning. The participants then make their way to the kitchen, where they're soon enjoying an especially bountiful and social-ly lively breakfast.

The rest of Sunday morning proceeds as usual with a program open to the public. During ango seasons, however, one of the teachers con-ducts a dharma combat rather than giving a talk. Basically, a dharma combat is a public form of dokusan, in which the teacher makes an opening statement and then challenges students to test their under-standing of that statement in a brief, face-to-face dialogue. Interested students line up in the center of the zendo and, one by one, step up to the teacher and speak for everyone to hear.

Sesshin as a whole offers participants—including all residents and preregistered nonresidents—the ideal environment for intensifying their zazen. It's also their only opportunity to have several face-to-face encounters with a teacher during a single week. Nonresidents who join the sesshin later in the week (usually an option) may have just one or two encounters, but for some of them it's the sole context in which they receive any such teaching. Sesshins are led either by Daido, Myotai, or

A row of sesshin participants engage in oryoki-style lunch. Each person's three nesting bowls, chopsticks, spoon, and spatula are precisely arranged on a folded cloth
place mat. Condiments are served in a small tray placed between each dining pair.
A server stands in the rear, attending the last pair of diners in the row.

Shugen, although usually two and sometimes all three of these teachers are present and active.

One of my most rewarding insights into the function of sesshin came from a talk given in 1996 by Shugen (or, to use his full name and title, Geoffrey Shugen Arnold, Sensei, Shugen being his dharma name, meaning "vigorous practice"). A resident of the monastery since 1986, he received full transmission from Daido in 1997. He is currently the monastery's training coordinator and operations manager, responsible for all aspects of monastery business.

In Shugen's talk, he challenged us with this question: "The word *sesshin* means to collect or unify the mind. Collect it from where, unify it with what?" Later, after discussing the agitation that the mind goes through in processing things dualistically (one-two, me-other, this-that, good-bad, like-dislike, yes-no), he said:

> We think thoughts are the problem, we think our thinking is the problem. The mind thinks! That is what it does and is meant to do. Would you really want to eliminate it? What kind of person would you be then? . . . [Sesshin] is making every thought a thought of enlightenment and an enlightened thought. Incredible power comes from that. Ceaselessly and consistently live "not two . . . not two . . . not two." Moment to moment, twenty-four hours a day. (Here and above: as reprinted in "What Is Sesshin?" *Mountain Record*, winter 1996, pp. 12–16)

Shugen's words helped me to see more clearly into an issue that had been bothering me for years: How can I possibly let go of *all* thoughts in zazen? Putting it in very crude terms, I began to understand that the problematic thoughts—the kind that bedeviled my zazen—had to do with *dualistic* thinking, not with thinking in general. Sesshin gives one greater scope to do zazen and, therefore, to approach a more original, collected, unified way of thinking. The result can be what is called waking up.

5

Teachers and Teachings

By your own efforts
Waken yourself, watch yourself,
And live joyfully.   —THE BUDDHA

So far in this book, my interviewees and I have tried to put into accessible language what it's like to spend time in a Zen environment, what surface-level sights, sounds, smells, tastes, textures, feelings, and thoughts you might encounter. The impacts of the overall experience on one's inner life defies such easy description. Much of the difficulty has to do with the intangible nature of spirituality, which, when tackled with words, so often translates into enigma, paradox, triviality, or abstruseness.

For example, whenever I try to cast an objective, journalistic eye on Zen Mountain Monastery, I'm reminded of Thomas Merton's half-serious, half-joking rhetorical question, "What good is a monk?" The real world is overwhelmingly materialistic, even corporate: a hardball arena of facts and figures where quantitative values, marketable products, and regulatory laws are all-important. In this pragmatic domain, a monk does, indeed, appear to be a pointless, powerless, downright eccentric figure.

By contrast, when we pass through the door of the smallest Zen monastery, we enter a world of faith, trust, intuition, and spirit. Here a monk can not only gain mastery over life and death but also serve as a uniquely dynamic catalyst for positive change in others. I've found that to be true of the monastics at Zen Mountain Monastery, and so have many other people, some of whom speak about this matter later in the chapter.

Through my practice as a student at the monastery, I've also learned to question more constructively the whole notion of what is real and to live more comfortably with the ambiguities of life that used to upset me and prompt me to behave irresponsibly. I'm more open to the unknown, the untried, the unresolved. Having followed the monastic schedule so often, I can now see a sacredness in every day and each of its parts. It doesn't matter so much to me whether I can control all that goes on or whether it turns out the way I might have hoped. Regardless, I feel more in charge of, and recharged by, what happens.

When you stay at the monastery, you inevitably sense various quantum effects in space and time that condition you to develop a more spiritual, less rationalistic attitude toward life. Sitting on my zabuton, for example, I've experienced the zendo as a vast, blissful universe and as a coffin-sized torture chamber. While I'm performing a service position in this same room, it can feel like the stage of a gigantic, packed theater where one may either fail abysmally or succeed gloriously. As I slip into it to sit alone in the middle of the night, it can seem like a humble shelter in the wilderness where I'm barely out of the elements but utterly safe and hidden.

I have invested so much of my mind, heart, and energy in activities inside the zendo that every time I look at it I see shimmers of myriad different realities. Along with the ones just indicated, I catch glimpses of a perch in the void, a labyrinth marked by a million miles of footsteps, a dazzling audience chamber, an operating room with blood on the floor, and, as mentioned earlier, a ship sailing across an uncharted ocean. In sum, it has given me a sensitivity to "richness of place" that I'm able to exercise in other environments as well.

Time at the monastery can also be experienced as a mystical union of the absolute and relative. During zazen and any other activity that you pursue with the focused mind of zazen, minutes can seem eternal, and hours can pass like a fleeting instant.

The very structure of each day at the monastery allows for the merging of the ordinary and the extraordinary. Unlike its average counterpart in secular society, the monastery day has a natural rhythm to it. You get up in time to witness the dawn, sit for a while to ground yourself, have a substantial breakfast, work while your energy is up, eat your biggest meal at the day's exact midpoint, work again for a while, have a light supper, sit when it's best to still yourself, and retire not long after dusk. Despite the day's commonplace routine, however, any moment of it can take on a supernatural quality, giving you a sudden insight into the past or future, or an ecstatic adventure that's seemingly outside of time altogether.

Yet another wondrous, spiritually nourishing dimension of time spent at the monastery has to do with engaging voluntarily in a fine-tuned approach to living that has survived in much the same state for centuries. It could never have lasted so long if it weren't well designed to help people lead more deeply satisfying lives, regardless of the economic, social, political, or technological conditions temporarily prevailing in the outside world.

To follow this traditional way of experiencing each day, hour, and moment is somehow to give yourself deeper roots as a human being. The past comes alive in the present. Simultaneously, you feel less like a product of the modern era alone and, as a result, less vulnerable to the ups, downs, ins, and outs of contemporary existence.

When you stay for an extended period of time at the monastery— a week, a month, or a year—your identity is enriched in other remarkable ways as well. The most fundamental shift is that you come to appreciate yourself as a sentient being, not merely a personality or even a person. This understanding helps you relate more intimately to all sentient beings and, therefore, lose some of the artificial barriers or manipulative attachments you've set up between yourself and others.

A further self-liberating aspect of monastery life is that your identity there is not so bound up in what you do. You are made to feel just as important as everyone else, and just as much your own self, whether you wind up cleaning toilets or helping the abbot set up a training program, and whether you do your job flawlessly or make mistakes. Because we're so accustomed to define ourselves and our personal worth in terms of our occupation, this simple, emancipating shift in self-concept can be profoundly gratifying.

A similar process is set in motion at the monastery by the practical use of different titles. For instance, if you stay for a month or longer, you are assigned a temporary service position (each one lasts at least a month). It comes with its own title: usher, first attendant, jikido, and so on. If the person in charge of supervising your position needs to talk with you about your performance or call your attention to something publicly, he or she uses your title, not your name.

Thus, assuming you're an usher and you forget to rearrange a certain zabuton just before morning service, you and the other sangha members gathered in the zendo will hear your supervisor cry out "Usher!" rather than your name. It may be a small difference, but it's a significant one: The role, not the individual, is being singled out.

Then there's the use of dharma names. Ever since I took Buddhist vows in 1996, I've had the dharma name Hosho, meaning "abundant blossoms." Here, again, is an example of receiving a title that doesn't tie down one's concept of self but, rather, expands it.

Dharma names are carefully chosen by one's teacher (in my case, Daido) to serve as teachings to their recipients. Like everyone else given a dharma name, I was told to think of mine as a koan, and so I continue to sit with the koan of Hosho. Sometimes I connect the image of "abundant blossoms" to the diamonds in Indra's net, that is, to the universe of sentient beings. But there are many other meanings I can read into the name as well, each of which is a means of identifying myself more intimately with the dharma.

No matter how briefly or long you visit a Zen monastery, you'll find that the most important lessons you learn are the ones you teach yourself. This brings up a very good question: How do you go about being your own teacher, no matter how much or how little you know about Zen practice?

The disarmingly simple answer lies in one of my favorite anecdotes from Zen history. The fifteenth-century Japanese Zen master Ikkyu was once asked by a student, "Can you write down on this parchment the highest teaching of Zen?" Ikkyu picked up a brush and wrote the word, "Attention." The student frowned. "But surely there's something more!" he said. "Yes, there is," replied Ikkyu, who picked up the brush again and wrote, "Attention." The student, unsatisfied, cried out, "Is that it?" Ikkyu responded, "No, there's more." Once again he picked up the brush and wrote, "Attention." As a result, the finished parchment read, "Attention. Attention. Attention."

Communal living at Zen Mountain Monastery provides me with ample opportunities to be attentive and many teachers to help me train myself in this practice. In addition to the formally transmitted teachers are all the other individuals with whom I come into contact again and again on a daily basis—people who are there searching for the same thing I seek, going through the same experiences I am, and, often, disclosing themselves as starkly as I reveal myself.

The net result of our group interaction is a mutual smoothing and polishing, as if we were all rocks being cleaned in a mill. Rough edges in our thoughts, words, and deeds are gradually knocked off. Our private tendencies to separate, to distinguish self from others, get slowly but surely rubbed down. The same kind of refining process can be found at Zen places throughout North America, because it's an inevitable byproduct of Zen practice in a group context.

Sometimes certain resonances develop between people at the monastery so that one person—knowingly or not—serves as a particularly significant role model or teacher for another. It may happen because of a personality match or an obvious counterbalance between one individual's skill, grace, or knowledge and the other's lack thereof. However, judging from my own experience and what people have told me, it's usually due to something more mysterious than that.

For example, you can become a teacher of this kind by having a special private appreciation for what someone else is going through and, in response, making more of an effort to engage that person in conversation and to support his or her strengths. The student in this kind of relationship may or may not know that your effort is an intentional one.

You may also become a teacher—or a role model—without ever being aware of it. The student who is inspired by your example of practice may or may not overtly seek a stronger relationship with you. Often simply having your example in mind is enough for the student.

I suspect that among the longtime sangha members at the monastery, the network of such relationships is so interwoven that every individual is at once a teacher, role model, and student vis-à-vis different members of the group. In some one-to-one connections, I'm sure, each individual is alternately a teacher, role model, or student of the other, depending on the circumstances. I know for a fact that many young people mentor older ones as well as vice versa.

Finally, there are the "teachings of the insentient," as they are known in Zen: That is, the things we can learn from inanimate objects, forms, and designs. These teachings are typically the most difficult to recognize, but they tend to stand out more in the context of a spiritual environment, where people's minds and hearts are more receptive to their subtle signals.

At Zen Mountain Monastery, as at other Zen places, much of what is taught by the insentient surroundings is about the interdependent nature of the everyday and the sublime, the concrete and the abstract, the absolute and the relative, the formal and the empty. You see it reflected at the monastery, for example, in the patterns of zafus and zabutons in the zendo; the knots in the pinewood floors; the panes in the window casements; the characters in the wall-mounted calligraphy; the mounds of chopped vegetables on the kitchen table; the stones in the buildings, gardens, walkways, and streams; the leaf shapes, barkscapes, and needle configurations in the bushes, trees, and forest; the light and shadow dapples on the lawn, walkways, and stairs; and the clouds, planets, and stars in the wide-open sky.

To allude to all the effects, roles, relationships, and images I've just cataloged is only to pause at the luminous threshold of the deeper teachings that are obtainable—not only at Zen Mountain Monastery specifically but also at authentic Zen places in general. In order to discover what kind of teachings these are, you need to enter into the life of a Zen monastery, center, or zendo and experience them yourself. Meanwhile, the rest of this chapter recounts what others tell me about the teachers and teachings they've encountered.

David: "destined to be here"

As a Vietnam War veteran and now a college football coach, David is not the kind of person you'd expect to believe in psychic phenomena. For the most part he doesn't, but he's convinced that some kind of mystical force brought him to Zen Mountain Monastery three years ago for a Zen training weekend.

"I felt destined to be here almost the moment I walked through the door," David recalls. "I saw a deep caring here that I'd been seeking for years, a real integrity, nothing sentimental, hip, casual, or holier-than-thou. It struck me as a place I needed to have in my life."

David had been hunting for a spiritual base ever since returning from Vietnam. "I'd had glimpses of Zen Buddhism while I was stationed in Nam," he says, "but that wasn't what made me start looking around for some sort of higher meaning in life. It was the awful suffering, corruption, and chaos that was everywhere there. After my discharge, I couldn't get that out of my head, so whenever I had the time, I'd travel around and check out places that might have some answers, that might be able to serve as a resource or a haven for me."

Since that Zen training weekend, David has returned here intermittently for sesshins and retreats but has not applied for student status. Because he lives in Ohio, the distance alone would make it difficult to develop a close relationship with his teacher and to meet the requirement of attending at least a part of a sesshin twice a year, but that isn't the reason he gives for not becoming a student. "Even if I lived around the corner," he insists, "I probably wouldn't do it. I'm not ready for that degree of commitment to a religion. I may never be. To me, it's enough that this place is here. It proves something to me about human potential."

Many aspects of the monastery appealed immediately to David because of his background as a soldier and a coach—yet another explanation for why he felt it was his destiny to arrive here. "I have a tremendous respect for the kind of effort they're making," he asserts. "The discipline, the commitment, the coming together as one—these are things I value. I sincerely think they represent the best and most natural tendencies in human beings. It's great to see them put to the task of furthering spiritual goals."

Although David appreciated the monastery atmosphere right from the start and found the people, in his words, "obviously sincere and easy to be with," he was shocked by how incompetent he felt while sitting zazen or trying to do caretaking jobs with a zazenlike mind. "I figured I'd take to all that like a duck to water," he remembers. "Maybe on some level I did, but I caught myself glancing at the other people around me and thinking, 'They're all much more buddhalike than I am!' It didn't occur to me that I might have appeared just as composed to them as they seemed to me. It wasn't until I talked with people afterward that I realized many of them, maybe all of them, were going through some of the same kind of internal crap that I was."

David's years of involvement with the monastery have exposed to him the self-limiting falseness of many of his lifelong assumptions regarding spiritual growth. "I used to associate 'seeing the light' with having some kind of orgasm of joy," he reveals. "Well, it can be like that, but it can also happen when you're depressed, desperate, or just plain quiet. I've also learned more not to put things into boxes like 'happiness is good, sadness is bad' or 'freedom is running through the fields and captivity is being confined to one place.' I'm better at experiencing things without overjudging them."

This lesson became especially palpable to him the first day of his first sesshin. "I felt an overwhelming sadness," he recalls, "and I couldn't understand why. I'd looked forward to this sesshin for months. Then it came to me like a flash—I was sad because whenever I was walking around, I was looking down at my feet and not speaking to anyone. I'd always linked that kind of behavior with sadness, and now it was automatically making me feel sad even though I had no real cause to. That was a big revelation, that I was functioning so automatically and not really consciously."

Other lessons David has learned have been more complex and have touched more profound issues in his life. "Over the years as I practice what I've been taught here," he confides, "I've taken on more and more responsibility for my life. It extends even to things like responsibility for what happened in Nam. That doesn't necessarily mean that I caused certain things to happen but that I need to assume responsibility for them, that somehow I need to acknowledge them and make something of them in my life."

What David has been taught or has taught himself also seems to have had a positive effect on his relationship with his wife. "She's been very good about my leaving her to come here every now and then," he says. "I don't think she really understands or buys into what I'm doing here. But she told me last week that now, when I *am* home, I'm more truly with her than I used to be."

Despite the fact that David doesn't get to the monastery often, he believes that he's absorbing its teachings "about as much as I'm able to, at a pace that's right for me." The best evidence he has that it's working for him is quite visceral: "The more I take the practice into my life," he claims, "the more eager I am to get up in the morning and the better I sleep at night."

Ryushin: "the most important thing to do"

Formerly a pediatrician and then a psychologist, Ryushin (his dharma name, meaning "dragon mind") is now a senior monastic at the monastery and, among other assignments, managing editor of Dharma Communications. As a teenager he emigrated from Poland to the United States with his mother and sister: an early indoctrination into changing worlds to achieve greater freedom. He went on to develop many intellectual interests and a taste for outdoor adventure, including sailing, skiing, and rock climbing. These were the things that eventually came to sustain his life as an adult.

Ryushin, then Konrad, first met Daido at a Buddhism and psychology conference in New York City and soon afterward came to the monastery for a sesshin. "I went through a lot of suffering at that sesshin, physically and emotionally," he admits, "but I also got a lot of comfort, support, and best of all, validation. The whole thing seemed like a confirmation of my own insanity."

If we accept the notion that "insanity" to an intellectual is the part of his or her mental life that doesn't make logical sense and, therefore, is especially disturbing, then we can better appreciate what Ryushin valued most about the sesshin: "It was not intellectual at all," he recalls. "Instead, it was about feeling."

Ryushin became a student at the monastery in 1988 and a resident four years later. "Prior to moving in here, I was working in a mobile crisis unit in Albany, a street clinic for the mentally handicapped," he says. "I was also staying in a house nearby and spending several days at the monastery during the week. It was a very solitary, independent existence, satisfying in many ways but with a palpable hollowness."

Ryushin had serious concerns about entering the monastery, but he didn't let them stop him. Indeed, as he describes it, he couldn't have. "I was worried about living in community here," he confesses, "but at the same time I was realizing that my life was in my hands. I was focusing more and more on just one question: What is the most important thing to do with my life? I knew that the answer was to come here. I felt there was no time to waste. I had to throw myself into it."

At first, just as Ryushin had anticipated, communal living posed some thorny dilemmas. "One of my worst problems was loneliness," he remembers. "There were plenty of people around me, but I was very unsocial. I lacked the skill of being spontaneous or open to them. I was also clinging to my own identity and dealing with a lot of anger. In fact, anger has always been an issue for me. I'm still in the process of learning how to harness it, how to make it function for the betterment of others."

Today, Ryushin can testify to positive changes in his frame of mind since those early days. "I continue to work with self-clinging," he comments, "and perhaps because of that I can experience difficulty entering into the liturgy wholeheartedly. At the same time I'm also aware that I've been moving continuously along a spiritual path of development, and that's quite surprising and humbling."

As for teachers and teachings, Ryushin emphasizes the significance in his life of his primary dharma teacher—that single most critical individual in any Zen student's education. "What I appreciate most now in my practice is the relationship I have with Daido," he asserts. "The intimacy of that mind-to-mind connection, the uniqueness of it, is astounding. I'm amazed at the capability of teaching and being taught in that way."

In a recent *Mountain Record* article, Ryushin, once again revealing himself as the intellectual-turned-Buddhist, cites one of his teacher's statements to describe what he himself has come to know as the meeting place of thinking and nonthinking, science and religion:

> Daido Roshi points out that each one of us is inherently a manifestation of a unified universe. In a sense, we don't need a unified theory. Each moment we experience is living proof of a completely interconnected time and space. Each moment can guide us inexhaustibly in our explorations if we are willing to listen with impeccable care and rapt attention; if we are willing to see this life-path with the eyes of wonder. ("No End to Our Exploration," *Mountain Record*, fall 1999, p. 20)

Michelle: "seeing the things I didn't before"

Michelle, currently finishing her second, one-year period of residency at the monastery, has a life history that speaks on the surface of courage, self-reliance, and spunk. Born in Brooklyn, she left as soon as she could drive for the mountains of Colorado and eventually wound up in Alaska. She's been an architect for eight years and before that took care of race horses.

Nevertheless, when Michelle first visited the monastery for a Sunday service, she was, in her own words, "wide awake with fear." It didn't help that she was late getting to Mt. Tremper from New York City, nor that she was anxiously looking forward to picking up her partner, who'd been staying here. "I was scared to death I'd do something wrong," she recalls. "I was so nervous that the greeter at the front door had to come out from behind her desk and walk me up to the zendo. 'Don't worry,' she kept telling me. 'You'll know what to do.' And, of course, I did."

Back home in Alaska, Michelle and her partner, both of whom had formerly practiced a looser style of Buddhist meditation, began sitting zazen. They even conducted their own personal sesshins, preparing food for oryoki in advance and asking people at work to respect their wish to remain as silent as possible. After a while, Michelle decided that she wanted to spend some time by herself at the monastery. That was three years ago.

The first few months, Michelle felt constrained to be pleasant all the time, no matter what was really going on inside her. "There's no place to hide here," she points out. "When I was sad, I'd put on a smiley face, or try to. Finally I realized I could just fall apart, that it was okay, that there was a safety net in the kind of people here and in the schedule. I was able to trust that I could recover, get right back into it, and not lose anything in the process."

Part of the breakthrough for Michelle was that she became more adept at seeing herself in others and vice versa. Referring to those initial months of struggle, she admits, "Now I know how obvious my pain must have been to everyone else, even though I was trying to conceal it. If you really look, you can tell how someone is feeling, especially if you're around the person a lot."

Michelle claims that one of the major lessons she's learned from life at the monastery has been to accept others more easily and compassionately. "When I first came here," she recalls, "suddenly I was living with all sorts of people I would never otherwise have lived with. I took comfort in the fact that everyone was here for the same reason, but still, every now and then, someone would really annoy me. Then, after a while, if someone was bothering me and I later saw that person in the zendo with me and everyone else, I'd get over it right away. That would be the end of my bad feelings about the person. It's one thing to know that the two of you have something in common. It's another to actually share that thing together so deeply and totally."

Michelle found the monastics to be very resourceful in helping her accommodate herself to life at the monastery. "I originally perceived them as authority figures," she notes. "It took me a while to ask them for help, but when I did, they turned out to be much more open and giving than I'd ever imagined."

The monastics also demonstrated to Michelle that they're capable of offering other, more far-reaching kinds of support. Toward the end of that first period of residence for Michelle three years ago, she was allotted the caretaking assignment several days in a row of designing a new bathhouse for the cabin residents to use. "I was convinced it was just a nice gesture," she said, "a means of getting me back into gear as an architect before I returned to my job in Alaska. I did give the drawing my full attention, but as far as I could tell, it was basically one of those hypothetical, back-of-an-envelope, wishful-thinking things. I had complete freedom to draw whatever I thought best, with no suggested materials or budget."

Nine months later, Michelle discovered the real truth. "I e-mailed the monastery from Alaska saying I wanted to come back for a stay," she explains, "and Ryushin replied, 'By the way, the bathhouse looks great.' I thought it was a joke, but there the bathhouse stands today. What trust they invested in me and my work! What project like that does an architect ever create that doesn't bring you sixty phone calls as it's being built?"

Michelle knows from personal experience that the same Zen lessons can recur again and again to be relearned again and again and, therefore, that a teacher remains ever essential in a student's life. "I can't imagine not coming back to the monastery on a regular basis," she declares. "The access to teachers at the monastery is phenomenal, and they keep you straight even when you have no idea you're wandering off somewhere."

Asked for a specific example, Michelle says, "I get down to the city at least once a month during hosan to see my family, and lately I've been noticing that we're really getting along much better. It's especially true of this one relationship I have that's always been difficult. I told Shugen, 'This guy is really changing! It's unbelievable!' Shugen said, 'You know, it's probably not this guy who's been changing. It's probably you.' I hadn't thought of that at all, but Shugen was absolutely right."

In general, Michelle has learned to be more tolerant not only of others but also of herself. "Sometimes I feel as if I'm doing worse than I did before I ever got into Zen," she confesses, "that I goof up more often or go crazy more easily. Then I realize it's just that my consciousness of such things is so much greater now. I see the things I didn't before, the little slips, the crises coming on. I'm 100 percent more aware now of how energy starts to change in my mind and my body."

Jinzan: "putting pressure on the self"

Many individuals are drawn to Zen not because they reject the faith in which they were raised but, rather, because they seek to extend the heart of that faith into another dimension. One of them is Jinzan (his dharma name, meaning "spirit mountain"), who was brought up Christian and is currently a resident at the monastery.

"Both Christianity and Zen emphasize unity," Jinzan maintains. "In Christianity the ideal is not to distinguish between little self and Big

God Self. There should be no separation. It's a unity that goes beyond our everyday understanding: You are not God, but God is all of you. Zen teaches the same thing in its way. I like the devotional aspects of Christianity, such as prayer, and I like the contemplative discipline and physiological training of Zen. In my religious practice, I try to let the two harmonize together."

The music metaphor is appropriate. For most of twenty years before coming to the monastery, Jinzan, then Parker, was a professional musician, playing his guitar in clubs across the United States and twenty-two other countries. Always in the back of his mind, however, was his love for Zen practice, and it brought him again and again to a Zen environment for spiritual renewal. He turned twenty years old while staying at Shasta Abbey, a Zen monastery in California. During another period of residence there, he turned thirty. He celebrated his fortieth birthday at Zen Mountain Monastery.

"When I first arrived here," Jinzan remembers, "I immediately sensed that there was real serious training going on. I'll admit I was intimidated for quite a long time, but instinctively I trusted everything about the place.

This confidence in the monastery was critical for Jinzan, because one thing that caused him a great deal of difficulty right away was the lack of say he had about his daily schedule. "In addition to having little choice about what you do here," he remarks, "you're doing something almost all the time."

Over the weeks and months, however, Jinzan came to regard this state of affairs as a freedom from choice rather than a lack of choice. "Being a resident," he says, "you have to do things here that would be too hard to do, or too hard to make yourself do, out in the world. And you choose to come here partly for that reason. It's a skillful way of putting pressure on yourself, so that what you most want to occur can and will occur. This place is supposed to be cooking you, and the people here are assuming you want to be cooked."

Jinzan refers to the example set by the senior monastics as a teaching that never ceases to impress, instruct, and motivate him. "When you're around here any length of time at all," he notes, "you realize that the seniors are more demanding on themselves than they are on other people. They get to the zendo earlier, sit longer, work harder, put themselves out there more. In the beginning they may seem stern, but scratch below the surface and there's a lot of joy, love, and tenderness underneath. At many other, less intense centers, it's the opposite."

According to Jinzan, a similar analogy applies to Zen practice at the monastery. "It's like working out at the gym," he claims. "If it hurts now, it will feel good later. If it feels good now, it will hurt later. That's almost guaranteed."

Jinzan currently attributes much of the initial difficulty he faced at the monastery to his own overreactions or misconceptions. "Life here is much more doable than you first think it is," he reports. "Often the problem is just that it's unusual. You can't rely on the same old things to get you through it. If you start to intellectualize about what's going on, you separate from it, and then things can start feeling more and more uncomfortable. But the discomfort is all in your mind. What's most helpful to me when I start separating that way is to remind myself of why I came here, of what I wanted to make happen. It's extremely important never to forget that."

Kaijin: "accepting things as they are"

Kaijin (her dharma name, meaning "ocean of purity") is the newest senior monastic at the monastery, but her life as a Buddhist has been one of the longest. Born in England, she lived for many years in New Zealand, where she worked as a nurse and studied Tibetan Buddhism. Eventually she began practicing with the Zen Institute of New Zealand and hearing about Zen Mountain Monastery, which has several affiliate sitting groups in that country. In 1994 she moved to the monastery with the intent of pursuing its monastic track.

Kaijin recalls that she was much more inwardly inclined to impose her will on things when she first entered into communal life here. "Before I came to the monastery, I lived in a horticultural community with seventy-five other residents," she says, "and I was one of the more opinionated people about how things should be done. If someone was creating problems for everyone else, I'd be the one saying, 'He has to go!' Here at the monastery, I've learned more to begin by accepting things as they are."

To illustrate her point, Kaijin tells a story: "Once the universe was divided into three parts—the Kingdom of the East, the Kingdom of the West, and between them, the Kingdom of Chaos. Whenever the King of the East and the King of the West needed to get together, they'd meet in the Kingdom of Chaos. After a while, these two kings wanted to give something to the King of Chaos to express their appreciation for allowing them to meet there. Wondering what to give him, it occurred to them that the King of Chaos had no physical characteristics. So they dug seven holes into the top of him to correspond to the seven holes in the human face. And what should happen, but the King of Chaos died of the wounds!"

Kaijin chuckles. "That story's been on my mind a lot lately," she says. "I think about it whenever I'm tempted to leap in and make something right!"

During her first couple of years at the monastery, Kaijin, then Mary, experienced many different challenges to her personal sense of rightness. "I was a bit paranoid then," she admits. "I was determined not to do anything that would make people want to get rid of me. Well, there were all sorts of unexpected complications. For instance, my first job was answering the phone, but I had trouble understanding the people who called because their accents and many of their words were new to me. My messages were usually too garbled to read. It was a disaster! Even when I walked through the halls, I'd be fumbling about. I'd try to pass people on the right, as it's done in New Zealand, and they'd try to pass me on the left, as it's done here."

Kaijin also took great pains then not to assert her own judgment but, rather, to take everyone's word at face value. When she was first put in charge of the vegetable garden at the monastery, she learned the danger of being too passive in this regard. Early in May she was told it was time to put indoor seedlings outside into the garden. Not being familiar with the seasons and some of the plants in this part of the world, she simply put all the seedlings into the ground, including the tomatoes—weeks before their time. When a frost was forecast one night, she labored long and hard to cover them with tarps, all the time fretting that she'd lose a big portion of the monastery's future food supply.

In the end, Kaijin managed to save most of the tomato plants. She also learned a valuable lesson in the "middle way" approach to life that's a core element of Buddhism. "It taught me not to trust in things blindly," she says. "It taught me not to be afraid to question things and not to be concerned about appearing ignorant or pushy, but to get all the information I need to do things well."

Despite the fact that Kaijin is now a senior monastic and the skilled supervisor of housekeeping as well as gardening, she draws a wealth of nourishment from observing and working with newcomers at the monastery. Perhaps it's because they keep her mindful of both her original motivation to practice and her early problems here. "The fact that people take it upon themselves to come to Zen Mountain Monastery is wonderful to me," she declares. "It astonishes me that they're so willing to try, and, in some cases, to travel such long distances, knowing so little about the place. It's taking a big risk."

Kaijin often witnesses the inspiring spectacle of retreatants struggling with their fear and then learning to overcome it. "This is a very strange environment to most people," she points out. "Naturally they're scared. They think that they have to move about like a robot, and they do move that way, because they're paralyzed to a certain degree. It's marvelous to see them realize that it's not a matter of being a robot, that letting yourself ease into things is an essential part of the practice. Over and over again this sight teaches me."

6

Beginning
Your Own Journey

The study of Zen is like drilling wood to make fire:
The wisest course is to forge ahead without stopping.

—MASTER HAKUIN

Before newly accepted students at Zen Mountain Monastery enter the zendo to be greeted officially by a waiting sangha, they pause at the threshold and read aloud a petition beginning, "I come here realizing the question of Life and Death is a vital matter." Whether or not you have a sense of what this question involves (it can easily take a lifetime's work), you may not consider your own reason for wanting to spend time in a Zen environment to be quite so lofty.

Maybe you simply think it would be a cool thing to do.

Perhaps you're just looking for something to soothe your troubled nerves.

Whatever you may initially think is your motivation, if you look more thoroughly into it, pondering it over a period of time without seeking or settling for quick answers, most likely you'll come up with increasingly serious and coherent life-and-death concerns.

For example, why do you think this experience in particular might be a cool thing to do? What in general do you think of as cool? What does this say about you? About your aspirations and fears? About the quality and meaning of your life?

Why do you think this experience in particular might soothe your troubled nerves? Why are they troubled? How often and how much have you felt this way in your life? What has genuinely seemed to help in the past? What concerns do your troubled nerves give you about the future?

In fact, to inquire into Zen is to begin what is meant to be a constant questioning process along these lines, one that brings you closer and closer to waking up. Master Dogen alludes to this basic truth in the *Shobogenzo:*

> *To study the Buddha way is to study the self.*
> *To study the self is to forget the self.*
> *To forget the self is to be enlightened by the 10,000 things.*

The quest can prove supremely valuable for you, as it has been for countless millions of others, but it hinges on how much of yourself you put into each and every step of it. With this in mind, I highly recommend that you start—or resume—conducting a serious self-examination before venturing into any Zen environment that's new to you. Ask yourself again and again, "Why am I heading in this direction? What do I most want to find?"

The more clearly and deeply you understand the forces that are motivating your present interest, the more profound and worthwhile the eventual experience will be. Once you're actually in the Zen place you've chosen, your knowledge of your reasons for being there will serve as your talisman, guide, and sustenance whenever you lose your way, confront a barrier, or come within sight of an opportunity.

On a more practical level, you can also help prepare yourself for the venture by learning more about Zen from the many related books, tapes, and periodicals now on the market (see appendix B: Recommended

Reading). Zen Mountain Monastery, for instance, offers books, tapes, and a periodical, *Mountain Record: The Zen Practitioner's Journal*, that are produced and distributed through its affiliate, Dharma Communications (see the monastery's listing in appendix A).

Questions to Ask about Zen Places

Besides asking yourself questions and bringing them to your own studies of books, tapes, websites, and periodicals, it's a good idea to pose questions to one or more authorized spokespeople at any Zen institution you're thinking about visiting. Listed below are guidelines for interviewing contact people at Zen monasteries, centers, or zendos.

The questions presented in the list have no clear-cut "positive" or "negative" answers. Pursuing them is just a matter of becoming better informed. For example, you may or may not want to visit—or ultimately be glad you visited—a small, relatively simple zendo rather than a big, formal monastery. Whatever you decide, it can well be worth your while to visit several different kinds of places to find out whether one type suits you better than another.

- First, investigate the background of the place. Do it not only by talking on the phone with someone who's authorized or equipped to answer your questions (your first item of inquiry) but also by reading any literature the place offers and researching the place in a Buddhist directory: for example, *The Complete Guide to Buddhist America* (Boston: Shambhala Publications, 1998). Here are some of the things you might want to find out:
  - How long has it been in existence?
  - What facilities does it have (for example, one room for sitting? A building of its own? Urban or rural)?
  - What different kinds of people go there (for instance, all kinds? Many people with no Zen background? Predom-

inantly formal students? Mostly people of Asian ancestry who were raised Buddhist?)?

- What teachers are available there? (See below for questions relating specifically to teachers.)

- With what Zen-related places is it affiliated in North America or elsewhere (especially in Asia)?

- What particular school of Zen does it represent? What specific Zen lineage?

- What services, programs, retreats, and residencies does it offer (especially for newcomers)?

- How are the following things incorporated into the schedule: zazen, kinhin, oryoki, art or body practice, work practice, free time?

- What teachers, staff members, experienced students, or other sources can you easily consult to answer any questions you might have?

- All other considerations being equal, choose a place to visit that's close to where you live, so that you'll be more disposed to go back to it on a frequent basis if you like it.

- Either beforehand or during your first visit, talk informally with other people who know the place. Assuming you're talking with individuals you trust (at least intuitively), ask them about their experiences and share any general questions you have.

- Look into the background and qualifications of the teacher(s). For each teacher, seek answers to these questions:

  - How is he or she authorized to teach?

  - Has he or she received formal transmission from another teacher?

  - What lineage(s) does he or she represent?

  - How long has he or she been actively teaching?

  - Does he or she speak English well? Teach through an interpreter?

- On what basis is he or she there: permanent, temporary, part-time, full-time, or occasional?
- In what contexts can you interact with, or learn from, him or her? Does he or she have any publications or tapes available?

Questions You May Be Asked

If you're hoping to spend a week or more at a Zen place or to attend a particular retreat or event that has special training significance (like a sesshin), you may be interviewed in advance by a staff member. The purpose of such a dialogue is to help both you and the interviewer determine if it's appropriate for you to come.

In some cases, the discussion may reveal to you that the experience is not, after all, what you imagined it to be. Instead, it may appear too demanding, open-ended, basic, or advanced. There may even be specific factors involved that, in your opinion, disqualify you: For example, more familiarity with Zen traditions or practices may be expected than you think you have.

In other cases, the staff member may decide that your motivation is too ambiguous, casual, or narrowly targeted for you to fit in comfortably with the other individuals there and with the required schedule. Perhaps you sound more as if you're looking for psychotherapy than spirituality. Maybe your responses show that you're intent on receiving more personal attention than the place can provide.

Alternatively, you may both come to realize that your projected visit has a very high possibility of being mutually beneficial. You may find yourself especially eager to participate in the schedule that's been described, and the staff member may recognize you as just the kind of person the place is seeking: someone with an inspiring "beginner's mind" who is open to the complete range of training opportunities available.

Whatever way the interview goes, the process itself is a valuable means of self-protection and information gathering for both parties. The overriding question at issue has already been mentioned at the beginning of this chapter: Why do you want to go there? Listed below are other questions you may be asked.

It's important to you and to the place you're contacting that you answer these questions—or similar ones—as honestly and generously as you can. There are no right or wrong responses, and no one answer is going to seal or ruin your chances. Rather, the interview as a whole will establish a picture. Whether or not that picture shows you in harmony with the place will most likely be obvious to both you and the staff member.

Also, remember that the interview is a two-way street. You can and should ask your own related or clarifying questions at the same time.

- What is your spiritual background?
- How long have you been interested in, or been practicing, Zen? How did you first learn about it? About this place? About this service, program, retreat, or residency?
- Are you meditating now? How long have you been meditating? What kinds of meditation have you practiced in the past? What has meditation been like for you?
- How committed are you to learning, or engaging in, Zen practice?
- What have your past experiences been in terms of committing yourself to spiritual practice? To education or training? To jobs or a career? To relationships?
- How willing are you to participate in every aspect of the schedule? Do we have your permission to train you according to what we believe is appropriate? Are you willing to live exactly as the others around you do? (If you're uncertain what is meant by this line of questioning, be sure to ask. Among the demands may be, for example, get-

ting up earlier in the morning than you usually do; eating a more restricted diet; sharing limited bathroom facilities; engaging fully in all scheduled activities, including liturgical and work practices; and doing without much privacy or solitary time.)

- What have your past experiences been in adjusting physically, mentally, and emotionally to similar kinds of services, programs, retreats, or residencies?

Regardless of how compassionately an institutional spokesperson conducts this probing kind of interview, it can seem very challenging and invasive. Bear in mind that it needs to take the relatively tough form it does. Once you're immersed in a Zen environment, these are precisely the kinds of questions you'll be forced to confront on your own, during face-to-face encounters with a teacher, and, perhaps, in conversations with other individuals there. In addition, those individuals will be making themselves vulnerable to the same sort of self-examination and scrutiny by others, and the interviewer has to be reasonably certain that your presence among them won't prove too incompatible or problematic.

A Few Final Words of Advice

Several of the Zen Mountain Monastery residents and visitors interviewed for this book have helpful suggestions to offer to people who are preparing for their first week-or-longer stay at any Zen monastery, center, or zendo. Most of their guidance balances pragmatic concerns with more abstract ones.

Drew, for example, counsels, "Bring your favorite sweatshirt, a supply of earplugs, work clothes, and a pair of shoes or slippers you can slip on and off easily. Also, know that you'll go through some strange mood swings, and be tolerant about that. For instance, you can serenely float up to your bed after the last sit of the day, certain that you're a little bodhisattva, and moments later want to kill someone who's making a lot of noise rummaging through a suitcase."

Kaijin is similarly practical as well as philosophical. "Do some reading about Zen," she recommends, "and practice sitting on a cushion for several days beforehand, even if it's just while you're watching TV. Also, be aware that the more rigid your expectations are, the more difficult your time will be. Once you're there, you'll need to put yourself into the experience and suspend judgment for a while, particularly idle complaints that will only feed your fears and resistance, like 'This is stupid!' or 'I'm being brainwashed!'"

Jinzan focuses more tightly on this type of attitudinal adjustment. "When you're staying at [a Zen place], you need to keep reminding yourself that you wanted to go there for your own benefit," he cautions. "You don't simply get things handed to you there, you have to make them happen for yourself. [The place] only gives you the environment and the tools."

Taking the same heart-of-the-matter approach, Troy conjures a very vivid and instructive image of what he believes anyone will encounter while staying at a Zen place and going through such intensive experiences as zazen and communal living. "You know, we all have that junk drawer at home," he says, "that place where we put everything we don't know what to do with. It's the same thing with our minds—we have a place where we store all the stuff we don't know how to deal with. Be prepared to have that mental junk drawer pulled out and turned over, so that everything inside scatters all around. Then you just have to take the time to pick each thing up, look at it, and say, 'Do I really want this anymore?' If you don't, let go of it. If you do, stop treating it like junk."

Advice naturally tends to collect around the darker possibilities of an experience. Let's now look at the brighter side of spending time at a

Zen monastery, center, or zendo. What good can come of it? Granted that you won't be able to reproduce the same schedule or intensity of practice back home, what might you be able to carry over from your stay to improve the quality of your ongoing life?

By common agreement among all my interviewees, the most precious and likeliest aftereffect, assuming you continue to practice at least some of what you learn, will be greater moment-to-moment mindfulness. We all tend to spend too much time dwelling on the past or the future, which, as both modern psychology and traditional Zen tell us, is the source of most of our fear, anxiety, depression, and anger. In doing so, we miss the present moment, which is to say we miss our life as it is actually being lived, when the most intense joys we can know are obtainable.

The Buddha himself told a parable that, among other things, expresses this truth. Once a man walking across a field saw a fierce tiger coming up behind him. He fled, but the tiger only increased his speed. Coming to the edge of a high cliff, the man grabbed the root of a wild vine that was growing there and swung down over the edge. Shaking with fright, he looked below him and saw another fierce tiger waiting for him to fall. Only that thin vine kept him from being eaten one way or the other.

Two mice—one black, one white—came out of their nest near the cliff's edge and began nibbling away at the root of the vine. As they chewed on relentlessly, the man spotted a luscious strawberry growing nearby on the cliff face. Holding on to the vine with one hand, he plucked the strawberry with the other.

How sweet it tasted!

A Directory of Zen Places

This appendix contains contact information for different kinds of Zen monasteries, centers, and zendos throughout the United States and parts of Canada. It's a selected list of places that are open to the broadest range of the general public and that facilitate a number of different Zen practices and programs.

Although many of the institutions listed below do not offer the same extensive range of activities and opportunities that are available at Zen Mountain Monastery, they all provide access to the core Zen experiences I describe in this book, including zazen, kinhin, and sesshin (or similar forms of intensive zazen).

Unless otherwise noted, the places on the list represent Japanese Zen. As indicated where appropriate, some places represent Korean Zen (in Korean, Son), which is slightly different in form but has many of the same basic elements.

The directory is only meant to give you a sampling of contacts within each geographical area. Many other Zen institutions exist, and the fact that a given one doesn't appear here is by no means a reflection of its quality or suitability for visitors. When talking with one of the listed contacts, you may want to ask about other places in areas where you live, work, and travel.

As with any directory, the details offered here can change at any moment, so be prepared to consult other sources if necessary. To find other Zen places in your area or in some other part of the country, check local community centers, holistic organizations, bookstores, and religious listings in periodicals, telephone books, and Chamber of Commerce records. The Internet may also offer useful information.

Each entry below includes phone number, address, and a few words of supplementary information. Because of several complicating factors—including space considerations here, the wide variety of organizational structures represented, and the fact that most of these places are still evolving—the supplementary information is not standardized in kind from entry to entry. Therefore, do *not* assume, for example, that a given institution does not offer daily zazen, a weekend service, or some other program if it isn't mentioned below.

Also, the term *affiliation* is used in these entries to cover any type of association between two organizations. It does not specifically identify either one as a headquarters, branch, or loose associate of the other. For clarification, contact the institution itself.

The directory is divided into sections referring to different geographical areas, as follows:

- Eastern United States (includes states east and south of the Appalachian Mountains)
- Central United States (includes states west of the Appalachians and east of the Pacific Rim states)
- Western United States (includes states bordering the Pacific Ocean, Alaska, and Hawaii)
- Canada

Within each section, entries are alphabetically organized first by state (or province), second by city, and third by the name of the Zen institution.

Eastern United States

Connecticut
The Living Dharma Center
P.O. Box 513, Bolton, CT 06043; (860) 742-7049
Various weekly practices, sesshins, retreat and residency programs.

New Haven Zen Center
193 Mansfield St., New Haven, CT 06511; (203) 787-0912
Korean Zen; retreats and residential programs.

Florida
International Zen Institute of Florida
3860 Crawford Ave., Miami, FL 33133; (305) 448-8969
Daily zazen, monthly retreats.

Georgia
Atlanta Soto Zen Center
1404 McLendon Ave. NE, Atlanta, GA 30307; (404) 659-4749
Daily zazen, Sunday service, sesshins, and various programs.

Kentucky
Furnace Mountain
Box 545, Clay City, KY 40312; (606) 723-4329
Korean Zen; rural retreat center; daily zazen and various retreat and
residential programs.

Louisiana
New Orleans Zen Temple
748 Camp St., New Orleans, LA 70130; (504) 323-7024
Daily zazen, regular retreats.

Maryland
Baltimore Zendo
P.O. Box 3514, Baltimore, MD 21214; (410) 254-5128
Weekly zazen, occasional sesshins, and classes.

Massachusetts

Cambridge Zen Center
199 Auburn St., Cambridge, MA 02139; (617) 576-3229
Korean Zen; daily zazen, numerous retreats.

Pond Village Zendo
P.O. Box 354, 42-44 Shore Rd., North Truro, MA 02652; (508) 487-2979
Daily zazen, periodic retreats.

New Jersey

Jizo-An Monastery
1603 Highland Ave., Cinnaminson, NJ 08077; (856) 786-4150
Residential and nonresidential training; daily zazen.

New York

Dai Bosatsu Zendo and Monastery
HCR 1, Box 171, Livingston Manor, NY 12758; (845) 439-4566
Affiliated with Zen Studies Society and New York Zendo; various
Sesshins, retreats, and residential programs.

Zen Mountain Monastery
P.O. Box 197, South Plank Rd., Mount Tremper, NY 12457; (845)
688-2228
Affiliates include Dharma Communications, Zen Center of New York
City, and numerous sitting groups in the United States.

First Zen Institute of America
113 East 30th St., New York, NY 10016; (212) 686-2520
Twice weekly zazen, monthly intensive programs.

New York Zendo
223 East 67th St., New York, NY 10021; (212) 861-3333
Affiliated with Zen Studies Society and Dai Bosatsu; daily zazen, Saturday service, regular weekend sesshins.

Village Zendo
15 Washington Pl., #4E, New York, NY 10003; (212) 674-0832
Affiliated with Zen Community of New York; daily zazen, various
sesshins.

Zen Center of New York City
500 State St. (Brooklyn), New York, NY 11217; (212) 642-1591
Affiliated with Zen Mountain Monastery; daily zazen, Sunday service, numerous retreats.

Rochester Zen Center
7 Arnold Park, Rochester, NY 14607; (716) 473-9180
Founded by Philip Kapleau, Roshi; wide range of programs.

North Carolina
Chapel Hill Zen Group
P.O. Box 16302, Chapel Hill, NC 27516; (919) 967-0861
Weekly zazen, various sesshins.

Rhode Island
Providence Zen Center
99 Pound Rd., Cumberland, RI 02864; (401) 658-1464
Korean Zen; numerous retreats.

Vermont
Vermont Zen Center
P.O. Box 880, Shelburne, VT 05482; (802) 985-9746
Regular zazen, sesshins, retreats.

Virginia
Blue Ridge Zen Group
4460 Advance Mills Rd., Earlysville, VA 22936; (804) 973-5435
Charlottesville zendo and country retreat center; daily zazen, Sunday service, various retreats.

Central United States

Arizona
Zen Desert Sangha
PO Box 44122, Tucson, AZ 85733; (520) 319-6260
Founded by Robert Aitken, Roshi; affiliated with Diamond Sangha.

Colorado

Zen Center of Denver
1233 Columbine St., Denver, CO 80206
Daily zazen, sesshins, and various retreat programs.

Illinois

Great Plains Zen Center
P.O. Box 3362, Barrington, IL 60011; (847) 381-8798
Regular zazen, sesshins, workshops.

Zen Buddhist Temple
1710 West Cornelia Ave., Chicago, IL 60657; (312) 528-8685
Korean Zen; Sunday services and various retreat programs.

Northwest Chicago Zen Group
1433 East Walnut Ave., Des Plaines, IL 60016; (846) 298-8472
Regularly scheduled zazen and sesshins.

Chicago Zen Center
2029 Ridge Ave., Evanston, IL 60201; (847) 475-3015
Affiliated with Rochester Zen Center; daily zazen and various
sesshins.

Udambara Zen Center
501 Sherman Ave., Evanston, IL 60202; (847) 475-3264
Urban zendo and Wisconsin country retreat; daily zazen, regular
sesshins, various programs.

Iowa

Iowa City Zen Center
226 South Johnson, #2A, Iowa City, IA 52245; (319) 354-1997
Daily zazen, Saturday program, various sesshins and retreats.

Kansas

Kansas Zen Center
1423 New York St., Lawrence, KS 66044; (785) 331-2274
Korean Zen; daily zazen, various retreats.

Michigan
Zen Buddhist Temple
1214 Packard Rd., Ann Arbor, MI 48104; (313) 761-6520
Daily zazen and various retreats.

Minnesota
Minnesota Zen Meditation Center
3343 East Calhoun Pkwy., Minneapolis, MN 55408; (612) 822-5313
Regularly scheduled zazen and sesshins as well as numerous retreats.

Missouri
Missouri Zen Center
220 Spring Ave., Webster Groves, MO 63119; (314) 961-6138
Daily zazen, Sunday service, periodic sesshins.

Nebraska
Nebraska Zen Center
3625 Lafayette Ave., Omaha, NE 68131; (402) 551-9035
Daily zazen, various sesshins, retreats, seminars.

Nevada
Mojave Desert Zen Center
901 El Camino Way, Boulder City, NV 89005; (702) 293-4222
Korean Zen; regular zazen and various retreats.

New Mexico
Albuquerque Zen Center
P.O. Box 4585, Albuquerque, NM 87196; (505) 268-4877
Daily and weekend zazen, various retreat programs.

Hidden Mountain Zen Center
216 Ninth St. NW, Albuquerque, NM 87102; (505) 248-0649
Regular zazen and monthly retreats.

Ohio

CloudWater Zendo
21562 Lorain Rd., Fairview, OH 44126; (440) 331-8374
Weekly zazen, Sunday service, zazen intensives, various programs.

Texas

Empty Sky
2100 North Spring St., Amarillo, TX 79107; (806) 383-3764
Affiliated with Diamond Sangha (Hawaii); weekly zazen and regular sesshins.

Utah

Kanzeon Zen Center
1274 East South Temple, Salt Lake City, UT 84102; (801) 328-8414
Daily zazen, Sunday service, regular sesshins.

Wisconsin

Milwaukee Zen Center
2825 North Stowell Ave., Milwaukee, WI 53211; (414) 963-0526
Daily zazen, various programs.

Western United States

Alaska

Anchorage Zen Community
2401 Susitna, Anchorage, AK 99517; (907) 248-1049
Sesshins several times a year.

California

Berkeley Zen Center
1931 Russell St., Berkeley, CA 94703; (510) 845-2403
Daily zazen, regular sesshins, and residential training.

Tassajara Zen Mountain Center
39171 Tassajara Rd., Carmel Valley, CA 93924; (415) 431-3771
Affiliated with San Francisco Zen Center; monastic training; residential and retreat center; open to the nonresident public April through September.

Newport Mesa Zen Center
711 West 17th St., Suite A-8, Costa Mesa, CA 92663; (714) 631-5389
Sunday evening program and monthly zazen intensives.

Dharma Zen Center
1025 South Cloverdale Ave., Los Angles, CA 90019; (213) 934-0330
Korean Zen; daily zazen and monthly retreats.

Rinzai-Ji Zen Center
2505 Cimmaron St., Los Angeles, CA 90018; (323) 732-2263
Daily zazen and monthly retreats.

Zen Center of Los Angeles
923 South Normandie Ave., Los Angeles, CA 90006; (213) 387-2351
Founded by Hakuyu Taizan Maezumi, Roshi; daily zazen, monthly sesshin, and a wide variety of programs.

Jikoji
12100 Skyline Blvd., Los Gatos, CA 95030; (408) 741-9562
Mountain retreat center; weekend sesshins.

Mount Baldy Zen Center
Box 429, Mount Baldy, CA 91759; (909) 985-6410
Residential retreat center.

Shasta Abbey
P.O. Box 199, 3612 Summit Dr., Mount Shasta, CA 96067; (916) 926-4208
Residential monastery and retreat center offering weekend to long-term training.

Zen Mountain Center
P.O. Box 43, Mountain Center, CA 92561; (909) 659-5272
Daily zazen, monthly sesshins, residential training.

Bay Zen Center
5600A Snake Rd., Oakland, CA 94611; (510) 482-2533
Affiliated with Ordinary Mind Zen School (Charlotte Joko Beck);
daily zazen, periodic sesshins.

Hartford Street Zen Center
57 Hartford St., San Francisco, CA 94114; (415) 863-2507
Headed by Zenshin Philip Whalen; daily zazen, occasional retreats.

San Francisco Zen Center
300 Page St., San Francisco, CA 94102; (415) 863-3136
Founded by Shunryu Suzuki, Roshi; affiliates include Green Gulch
Farm and Zen Center and Tassajara Zen Mountain Center; daily
zazen, many different programs.

Santa Cruz Zen Center
115 School St., Santa Cruz, CA 95060; (831) 457-0206
Daily zazen, periodic sesshins.

Green Gulch Farm and Zen Center
1601 Shoreline Highway, Sausalito, CA 94965; (415) 383-3134
Affiliated with San Francisco Zen Center; daily zazen, Sunday service,
Regular sesshins, numerous retreat programs.

Middlebar Monastery
2503 Del Rio Dr., Stockton, CA 95204; (209) 462-9384
Daily zazen, various residence programs.

Mountain Spirit Center
8400 Juniper Way, Tehachapi, CA 93561; (661) 333-7204
Korean Zen; rural facility with various retreat programs.

Hawaii

Koko An Zendo
2119 Kaloa Way, Honolulu, HI 96822; (808) 946-0666
Headed by Robert Aitken, Roshi, founder; contact address is for all
centers of the Diamond Sangha, which also includes Maui Zendo and
Palolo Zen Center.

Zen Center of Hawaii
P.O. Box 2066, Kamuela, HI 96743; (808) 885-6109
Daily zazen and monthly sesshins.

Oregon
Zen Community of Oregon
P.O. Box 310, Corbett, OR 97019; (503) 695-2103
Portland center and country retreat center; weekly zazen and various
retreat programs.

Dharma Rain Zen Center
2539 Southeast Madison St.; Portland, OR 97214; (503) 239-4846
Daily zazen, various classes and retreats.

Washington
Dai Bai Zan Cho Bo Zen Temple
7700 Aurora Ave. North, Seattle, WA 98103; (206) 328-3944
Daily zazen, regular sessions, various programs.

One Drop Zendo
135 North 75th St., Seattle, WA 98103; (206) 784-1977
Seattle zendo and retreat center on Whidbey Island; weekly zazen,
regular sesshins.

Canada

British Columbia
Lions Gate Buddhist Priory
1745 West 16th Ave., Vancouver, BC V6J 2L9; (604) 738-4453
Affiliated with Shasta Abbey (California); weekly meditation, monthly retreats.

Victoria Zen Centre
4965 Cordova Bay Rd., Victoria, BC V8Y 2K1; (604) 658-5033
Urban zendo and mountain retreat; weekly zazen, various sesshins.

Nova Scotia
Wolfville Zazenkai
P.O. Box 96, Wolfville, NS B0P 1X0; (902) 542-1728
Affiliated with Zen Centre of Ottawa (both part of White Wind Zen
Community); weekly sittings, occasional retreats.

Ontario
Mountain Moon Sangha
939 Avenue Rd., #10, Toronto, ON M5P 2K7; (416) 485-7659
Weekly zazen, various zazen intensives, lectures, instruction.

Zen Centre of Ottawa
240 Daly, Ottawa, ON K1N 6G2; (613) 562-1568
Affiliated with Wolfville Zazenkai in Nova Scotia (both part of White
Wind Zen Community); monastic training, monthly talks, various
sesshins and retreats.

Toronto Zen Centre
33 High Park Gardens, Toronto, ON M6R 1S8; (416) 766-3400
Daily zazen, regular sesshins, talks.

Quebec
Centre Zen de la Main
30 Rue Vallieres, Montreal, PQ H2W 1C2; (514) 842-7367
Daily zazen, various retreats; French and English spoken.

Montreal Zen Centre
824 Park Stanley, Montreal, PQ H2C 1A2; (514) 388-4518
Daily zazen, various retreats.

Recommended Reading

To learn more about basic Zen principles and practices, or to refresh your understanding of them, I recommend any of the books listed below as a good follow-up to this one. Each book is written by a modern teacher who helps bridge the gap between traditional doctrine and contemporary life. Because each individual writer's perspective can be so uniquely rewarding—a reflection of the fact that Zen truth arises from personal experience—you can easily read all of these works without feeling they are too repetitious.

This is a selected list to get you started. Other people who are knowledgeable in the field may suggest Zen books not mentioned here that are equally worthwhile. For some of the entries, alternative editions are available besides the one cited.

Enter anywhere and enjoy yourself!

Aitken, Robert. *Taking the Path of Zen*. San Francisco: North Point Press, 1982.

Beck, Charlotte Joko. *Everyday Zen: Love and Work*. San Francisco: Harper & Row, 1989.

Glassman, Bernard. *Instructions to the Cook: A Zen Master's Lessons in Living a Life That Matters.* New York: Bell Tower, 1996.

Harada, Sekkei. Translated by Daigaku Rumme. *The Essence of Zen.* New York: Kodansha International, 1992.

Kapleau, Philip. *The Three Pillars of Zen.* New York: Weatherhill, 1965.

Katagiri, Dainin. *Returning to Silence: Zen Practice in Daily Life.* Boston: Shambhala Publications, 1988.

Loori, John Daido. *The Eight Gates of Zen.* Mt. Tremper, N.Y.: Dharma Communications, 1992.

Maezumi, Hakuyu Taizan, and Bernard Tetsugen Glassman. *The Hazy Moon of Enlightenment.* Los Angeles: Center Publications, 1977.

Smith, Jean. *The Beginner's Guide to Zen Buddhism.* New York: Bell Tower, 2000.

Suzuki, D. T. *Manual of Zen Buddhism.* New York: Grove Weidenfeld, 1960.

Suzuki, Shunryu. *Zen Mind, Beginner's Mind.* New York: Weatherhill, 1970.

Uchiyama, Kosho. Translated by Shohaku Okumura and Tom Wright. *Opening the Hand of Thought: Approach to Zen.* New York: Penguin, 1993.

Chants and Precepts

The following chants and precepts used at Zen Mountain Monastery were formulated by the monastery from traditional texts.

The Heart Sutra

A sutra is a traditional text of Buddhist teachings. The following sutra, the centerpiece of the *Prajnaparamita Sutra* (hence its name), is chanted daily in virtually every Mahayana (including Zen) and Vajrayana temple and monastery throughout the world. At Zen Mountain Monastery, it is chanted during morning service. In the sutra, Avalokiteshvara, the bodhisattva of compassion, expresses to Shariputra, one of the Buddha's disciples, the fundamental doctrine of emptiness and form pervading the universe.

> Avalokiteshvara Bodhisattva, doing deep *prajna paramita* [practice of the highest wisdom], clearly saw emptiness of all the five conditions, thus completely relieving misfortune and pain.

173

"O Shariputra, form is no other than emptiness, emptiness no other than form. Form is exactly emptiness, emptiness exactly form. Sensation, conception, discrimination, awareness, are likewise like this.

"O Shariputra, all dharmas are forms of emptiness: not born, not destroyed, not stained, not pure, without loss, without gain. So in emptiness there is no form: no sensation, conception discrimination, awareness; no eye, ear, nose, tongue, body, mind; no color, sound, smell, taste, touch, phenomena; no realm of sight, no realm of consciousness, no ignorance and no end to ignorance, no old age and death and no end to old age and death, no suffering, no cause of suffering, no extinguishing, no path, no wisdom, and no gain.

"No gain and thus the bodhisattvas live, with no hindrance in the mind: no hindrance, therefore no fear.

"Far beyond deluded thoughts, this is nirvana.

"All past, present, and future buddhas live prajna paramita and therefore attain *anuttara-samyaksambodhi* [perfect universal enlightenment]."

Therefore know prajna paramita is the great mantra, the vivid mantra, the best mantra, the unsurpassable mantra.

It completely clears all pain.

This is the truth, not a lie.

So set forth the Prajna Paramita mantra, set forth this mantra and say, "Gate! Gate! Paragate! Parasamgate! Bodhi Svaha!" ["Further! Further! To the farthest (shore)! Beyond! Enlightenment, hail!"]

Prajna Heart Sutra.

Sho Sai Myo Kichijo Dharani

A dharani is a short sutralike work consisting of fundamental sounds that do not carry an extrinsic meaning. This particular dharani, widely used in Mahayana (including Zen) Buddhism, is associated with healing and is chanted at Zen Mountain Monastery during morning service.

> No mo san man da moto nan oha ra chi koto sha sono nan to ji to en gya gya gya ki gya ki un nun shiu ra shiu ra hara shiu ra hara shiu ra chishu sa chishu sa chishu ri chishu ri sowa ja sowa ja sen chi gya shiri ei somo ko.

The Meal Gatha

A gatha is a short sutralike text that encapsulates Buddhist teachings, usually as appropriate to a certain activity or occasion. This is the meal gatha chanted before breakfast and lunch at Zen Mountain Monastery.

> First, seventy-two labors brought us this food; we should know how it comes to us.
> Second, as we receive this offering, we should consider whether our virtue and practice deserve it.
> Third, as we desire the natural order of mind to be free from clinging, we must be free from greed.
> Fourth, to support our life we take this food.
> Fifth, to attain our way we take this food.
> First, this food is for the three treasures.
> Second, it is for our teachers, parents, nation, and all sentient beings.
> Third, it is for all beings in the six worlds.
> Thus, we eat this food with everyone.
> We eat to stop all evil, to practice good, to save all sentient beings, and to accomplish our buddha way.

The Ten Grave Precepts

The precepts are moral and ethical guidelines that one agrees to follow as a Buddhist. They are formulated somewhat differently in different Buddhist schools and institutions. The ten grave precepts used at Zen Mountain Monastery feature an unusual combination of both positive and negative expressions for each precept.

- Affirm life; do not kill.
- Be giving; do not steal.
- Honor the body; do not misuse sexuality.
- Manifest truth; do not lie.
- Proceed clearly; do not cloud the mind.
- See the perfection; do not speak of others' errors and faults.
- Realize self and other as one; do not elevate self and blame others.
- Give generously; do not be withholding.
- Actualize harmony; do not be angry.
- Experience the intimacy of things; do not defile the three treasures.

Glossary

Unless otherwise indicated in brackets or in the text, all non-English words and expressions in this glossary are in the Japanese language.

Because Zen is a branch of Mahayana Buddhism, terms general to Buddhism are usually given in Sanskrit, the liturgical language of Mahayana and Vajrayana Buddhism, rather than Pali, the closely related liturgical language of Theravada Buddhism.

For the sake of easy reading, no diacritical marks are included in Japanese or Sanskrit words.

Absolute/relative: In Mahayana Buddhism (including Zen), perfectly interrelated aspects of the universe. Absolute refers to oneness, emptiness, or true nature; relative, to its manifestation in different phenomena. A commonly recited sutra in Zen monasteries, centers, and zendos has the English title "The Identity of Relative and Absolute."

Anatman [Sanskrit]: literally, "no self"; one of the main doctrines of Buddhism, stating that there is no permanent, enduring entity known as the self or soul.

Ango: literally, "peaceful dwelling"; in Zen, a seasonal period of intensified spiritual training each year.

Anuttara-samyaksambodhi [Sanskrit]: the supreme, perfect enlightenment of a complete buddha: a phrase used, among other places, in the *Heart Sutra* (see p. 173).

Avalokiteshvara [Sanskrit]: in Mahayana (including Zen) and Vajrayana Buddhism, the transcendent or archetypal bodhisattva of compassion, viewed in some schools as male and in others as female; also known as Kannon or Kanzeon (Japan), Kuan Yin (China), and Chenrezig (Tibet).

Bodhi [Sanskrit]: literally "awakened." The bodhi mind is the enlightened mind. The bodhi tree is the name given to the sisal (fig) tree under which the Buddha attained enlightenment. The town in India where this occurred is now called Bodh-gaya in his honor.

Bodhidharma [Sanskrit; in Japanese, Bodhidaruma or Daruma] (c. 470–540 CE): the first patriarch in the Ch'an tradition of China and subsequent Zen tradition of Japan.

Bodhisattva [Sanskrit]: literally "enlightenment being." In Mahayana (including Zen) and Vajrayana Buddhism, the ideal practitioner: one who follows the buddha way and compassionately postpones final enlightenment for the sake of helping others realize themselves. The historical Buddha, Shakyamuni, as he was called, was also a bodhisattva. The word can additionally refer to transcendent or archetypal buddhas (see *Trikaya*).

Buddha [Sanskrit; in Japanese, butsu]: literally, "awakened one." A term that can be applied to anyone who attains full enlightenment, it is most widely known as a title for the historical Buddha. In Mahayana (including Zen) and Vajrayana Buddhism, it can additionally be applied to transcendent or archetypal buddhas (see *Trikaya*).

Buddha-dharma [Sanskrit]: the religion of the awakened one; the expression used in Asia for what Westerners call "Buddhism."

Buddha nature: In Mahayana (including Zen) and Vajrayana Buddhism, the eternal principle in each sentient being that makes him or her inherently capable of becoming enlightened (or, in other words, being a buddha).

Chado: the Zen art of tea: making the tea and serving it in a mindful manner according to a traditional protocol.

Ch'an [Chinese; in Japanese, Zen]: literally, "meditation"; the name of the Mahayana Buddhist school that emphasizes the practice of meditation.

Daiosho: literally, "great priest"; a title given to Zen masters, usually after they're dead.

Daisan: formal, face-to-face encounter between a Zen teacher and student (see *Dokusan*).

Dana [Sanskrit]: voluntary giving, one of the major virtues or perfections in Buddhism (see *Paramitas*).

Densho: the large bell at a Zen monastery, center, or zendo.

Deva [Sanskrit]: a godlike being who dwells in the highest of the six realms of existence.

Dharani [Sanskrit]: a short sutra consisting of basic sounds that have no explicit meaning.

Dharma [Sanskrit]: In Zen, the word *dharma* can be generally applied to mean the law or way of the universe or all phenomena in the universe. In a more specific sense, it refers to the teachings of the Buddha—the second of the three treasures in Buddhism, the other two being Buddha and sangha.

Dharma combat: see *Sosan*.

Dharma discourse: see *Teisho*.

Dharma name: Buddhist name given to a student by the teacher during the ceremony in which the student takes the precepts or, in other words, formally embraces Buddhism as a religion (see *Jukai*).

Dharma successor: a Zen student who has been recognized by his or her teacher as having received a comparable degree of enlightenment and, therefore, who has been given transmission: that is, permission to carry on the same line of teaching (see *Inka*).

Dharmakaya [Sanskrit]: in Mahayana (including Zen) and Vajrayana Buddhism, the eternal or truth body of a buddha (see *Trikaya*).

Diamond Sutra [in Sanskrit, *Vajrachchedika-prajnaparamita-sutra*]: one of the major Mahayana (including Zen) and Vajrayana Buddhist scriptures.

Doan: principal instrumentalist during Zen services in a zendo.

Dogen (also Eihei Dogen, Dogen Zenji, or Master Dogen; 1200–1253): one of the most prominent Japanese Zen masters and the founder of the Soto school in Japan. His compilation of dharma discourses, *Shobogenzo,* is regarded as a masterpiece in Buddhist literature.

Dojo: a room or hall in which one of the trainings related to Zen is practiced, for example, kendo (the way of the sword) or kyudo (the way of the bow).

Dokusan: formal, face-to-face encounter between a Zen teacher and student; a context for koan study as well as other forms of individual instruction. In some monasteries where an abbot and other teachers reside, only the encounter with the abbot is called a dokusan; encounters with the other teachers are called daisans.

Dragon: the English translation of the term used in Zen to refer to an enlightened being, as opposed to a snake or deluded being.

Duhkha [Sanskrit]: suffering, unsatisfactoriness. The first noble truth of Buddhism is that all life is suffering (see *Four noble truths*).

Eightfold Path, Noble: as stated in the fourth noble truth, the path to enlightenment, consisting of eight parts: right understanding, right thought, right speech, right action, right livelihood, right effort, right mindfulness, and right concentration.

Emptiness: see *Shunyata.*

Enlightenment: based on the Sanskrit term for awakening, the mind's heightened awareness of the self as an empty illusion, bringing with it a realization of oneness with the universe. The teachings of Buddhism are based on the Buddha's enlightenment and are designed to facilitate the student's own enlightenment.

Enso: the circle as a symbol of enlightenment, common in Zen painting; traditionally executed with a single, fluid brushstroke.

Five conditions/aggregates: see *Skandhas.*

Four noble truths: Also formulated as the four wisdoms, as revealed to the Buddha during his enlightenment: (1) all life is suffering; (2) the cause of suffering is desire; (3) suffering can be ended; (4) the way to end suffering is the Noble Eightfold Path.

Gassho: the Zen term for an ancient expression of greeting, gratitude, and reverence throughout Asia: a slight bow made with palms placed together.

Gatha [Sanskrit]: short sutra that presents a dharma teaching in a concise form, which, among other things, is suitable for chanting or reciting.

Gautama [Sanskrit]: the Buddha's surname or family name.

Genjokoan: literally, "the way of everyday life"; the first fascicle, or short essay, in Master Dogen's *Shobogenzo* and an important Zen teaching.

Haiku: a Zen form of poetry expressing the essence of a subject in seventeen syllables.

Han: resonant board, hung from ropes, that is struck to summon people in a Zen monastery, center, or zendo to events, including zazen sessions.

Hara: the spot approximately two inches below the navel that represents an individual's physical and spiritual center; in Zen, a source of energy for meditation and other forms of practice.

Heart Sutra (in Sanskrit, *Mahaprajnaparamita-hridaya-sutra*): the most widely chanted sutra in Mahayana (including Zen) and Vajrayana Buddhism; so named because it concisely articulates the core doctrine of emptiness conveyed in the larger sutra compilation called the *Prajnaparamita-sutra* (for the text as used in Zen Mountain Monastery, see p. 173).

Hosan: in a Zen monastery, period of time off from the monastic schedule: traditionally, every fifth day or every day with a 4 or a 9 in the date, but in some cases two consecutive days each week.

Hossu: a fly whisk or short staff with animal hair attached to one end, used by ancient monks to shoo insects without killing them; in Zen, passed as a symbol of mind-to-mind transmission from a teacher to his or her successor.

Ikebana: the Zen art of flower arrangement.

Inka: in Zen, a teacher's official confirmation that a student has completed his or her training with that teacher, which entitles the student to become a teacher on his or her own.

Ino: the chant leader during Zen services or ceremonies.

Jikido: the timekeeper for a Zen monastery, center, or zendo; among other tasks, the bell ringer to begin and end periods of zazen.

Jizo: the archetypal bodhisattva of benevolence and mercy, special protector of children, travelers, and people gone astray.

Joriki: literally, "mind power;" the mental, physical, and spiritual energy built up by zazen.

Jukai: literally, "receiving the precepts": in Zen, the ceremony of taking vows and receiving the precepts that represents a person's formal entry into Buddhism.

Kalpa [Sanskrit]: a vast amount of time, variously used as a unit to measure the time between the earthly appearances of a buddha, or on a larger scale, a whole world cycle.

Kanji: character(s) used in Japanese calligraphy.

Karma [Sanskrit]: the law of cause and effect, that is, that every thought or deed has a consequence that leads to another thought or deed, and so on; a key concept in all schools of Buddhism.

Karuna [Sanskrit]: compassion, one of the major Buddhist virtues; in Mahayana (including Zen) and Vajrayana Buddhism, embodied in the archetypal bodhisattva, Avalokiteshvara.

Kashyapa [Sanskrit] (also Mahakashyapa; in Japanese, Kasho): one of the Buddha's foremost disciples and the convoker of the first Buddhist Council after the Buddha's death; according to Zen, the only disciple who received transmission from the Buddha himself.

Kendo: the way of the sword: a Zen art.

Kensho: literally, "seeing [one's] nature"; in Zen, a sudden awakening or enlightenment experience.

Kesa: a monk's outer robe, worn across the shoulder.

Ki: the vital life force (in Chinese, *ch'i*) permeating all things; the energy tapped in the creative process.

Kinhin: in Zen, walking meditation, usually practiced between periods of zazen.

Koan: in Zen, a paradoxical teaching question or story designed to confound linear, rational thought and, therefore, to help condition the mind for enlightenment. Typically, a Zen student sits with a koan during zazen.

Kyosaku: literally, "wake-up stick"; a flattened stick used by zendo monitors to strike acupressure points on a person's shoulders, thereby relieving achiness and promoting wakefulness.

Kyudo: the art of archery, one of the Zen ways of practice.

Lin-chi (Chinese master, d. 867[?]): in China, founder of the Ch'an school named after him, which, in Zen, is called the Rinzai school and features koan study.

Lotus Sutra [in Sanskrit, *Saddharmapundarika-sutra*]: one of the major sutras in Mahayana Buddhism (including Zen).

Mahakashyapa: see *Kashyapa*.

Mahayana: literally, "great vehicle"; a major branch of Buddhism that arose during the first century CE in opposition to the more conservative Theravada ("way of the elders") branch. While the Theravada ideal is the scholarly, monastic, self-perfected arhat, the ideal in Mahayana, which aims at broader appeal to laypeople, is the bodhisattva, the one who postpones his or her own liberation in order to save all other sentient beings.

Maitri [Sanskrit]: kindness or loving-kindness; one of the major Buddhist virtues.

Manjushri [Sanskrit]: the archetypal bodhisattva of wisdom.

Mantra [Sanskrit]: an especially powerful syllable, word, or series of syllables or words used as a basis for chanting or meditation.

Middle way: the avoidance of extremes, a primary doctrine of Buddhism. Relating specifically to the life of the Buddha, it refers to the avoidance of either a life devoted to sensual pleasure or a life devoted to asceticism.

Mokugyo: literally, "wooden fish"; a hollowed-out, rounded wooden block resembling a sea creature that is used as a drum to pace the chanting during a Zen service.

Mondo: a question-and-answer session between a Zen master and his or her student(s); intellectual or conversational in manner, as opposed to other forms of face-to-face or public teaching.

Mu: literally, "nothing"; in Rinzai Zen, the name of one of the most well known beginning koans. Students sit with it in zazen (sitting meditation) in order to condition their minds for awakening. A fuller version of the koan is: "A monk asked Master Joshu, 'Does a dog have buddha nature?' Joshu replied, 'Mu.' What is Mu?"

Mudra [Sanskrit]: literally, "sign"; a certain posture of the hands that has a symbolic meaning. For example, in the zazen or cosmic mudra, the fingers of the left hand rest on top of the fingers of the right hand and the two thumbs lightly touch each other, forming an oval.

Nirmanakaya [Sanskrit]: in Mahayana (including Zen) and Vajrayana Buddhism, the form body of a buddha (see *Trikaya*).

Nirvana [Sanskrit]: literally, "extinguished"; the state of freedom from the cycle of birth-death-rebirth (*samsara*), which is a goal of enlightenment; oneness with the universe; sometimes used very broadly as a synonym for *shunyata* (emptiness).

Oryoki: literally, "just enough"; ceremonial eating with special bowls, practiced in Zen monasteries and centers and considered a Zen art or way by many authorities.

Osho: the title given to a Zen priest: the initial phase of transmission.

Pali: a dialect of Sanskrit; the liturgical language of Theravada Buddhism.

Paramitas [Sanskrit]: the perfections or virtues cultivated by Buddhists. In most schools, there are six, including generosity, discipline, patience, exertion, meditation, and wisdom.

Patriarch: in Ch'an and Zen, the succeeding masters in a teaching lineage.

Prajna [Sanskrit]: wisdom, one of the major Buddhist virtues. In Mahayana (including Zen) and Vajrayana Buddhism, it is embodied in the archetypal bodhisattva, Manjushri. The phrase *prajna paramita* means "highest wisdom."

Precepts: the principles of conduct that Buddhists agree to apply to their lives, often taken as vows on becoming a Buddhist (in Zen, during a Jukai ceremony) and always taken on being ordained as a monastic. The specific number of precepts and the words used to express them vary from school to school and context to context, but a common formulation is five precepts as follows: (1) avoid causing harm to other sentient beings; (2) avoid taking anything that is not freely given; (3) avoid sexual misconduct; (4) avoid untruthfulness; and (5) avoid clouding the mind with drugs. For the precepts followed at Zen Mountain Monastery, see page 176.

Rakasu: in Zen, a rectangular, biblike piece of clothing made of patches that symbolizes the Buddha's robe and is worn by monks and laypeople after taking Buddhist vows (see *Jukai*).

Rioban: special seating area in the zendo reserved for monastics, and, possibly, high-ranking lay practitioners.

Roshi: literally, "old [or revered] master"; in Zen, a monk who has received transmission and functions as a teacher. Properly, the title is only conferred to honor a very distinguished and experienced teacher, such as an abbot or head of a school.

Samadhi [Sanskrit]: mental firmness, clarity, or "one-pointedness" (as opposed to distraction or dualistic thinking).

Sambhogakaya [Sanskrit]: in Mahayana (including Zen) and Vajrayana Buddhism, the bliss body—or archetype—of a buddha or bodhisattva (see *Trikaya*).

Samsara [Sanskrit]: the cycle of birth-death-rebirth, characterized by suffering; the world of phenomenal things.

Sangha [Sanskrit]: community; the third of the three treasures of Buddhism (along with Buddha and dharma); strictly, the local community of monastics; more generally, any of the following: the local community of monastics and laypeople or all Buddhists or all sentient beings.

Satori: literally, "to know"; in Zen, enlightenment, often of a sudden nature; sometimes used as a synonym for *kensho*, although satori more properly applies to a more profound kind of awakening or the awakening of a buddha or bodhisattva.

Seiza: traditional Japanese way of sitting, with buttocks resting on heels; position using bench that can be adopted for zazen.

Sensei: title given to a Zen teacher who has received full transmission.

Sesshin: literally, "collecting the mind"; in Zen, a period of time (typically a week or ten days, but sometimes shorter or longer) when a monastery or center devotes more hours than normal per day to meditation. Often it is a regular event in the monthly calendar and features special talks as well as increased opportunities for face-to-face teaching.

Shakuhachi: the traditional Japanese bamboo flute, the playing of which is considered a Zen art.

Shakyamuni [Sanskrit]: literally, "sage of the Shakya clan"; title give to the historical Buddha, Siddhartha Gautama, after he left his father's court and went on his search for enlightenment.

Shariputra [Sanskrit]: one of the principal disciples of the Buddha; directly addressed in the *Heart Sutra* (see p. 173 in appendix C).

Shikantaza: literally, "nothing but sitting"; in Zen, meditation without any added techniques such as counting the breath or koan study.

Shobogenzo: literally, "Treasury of the True Dharma Eye"; the masterwork of Dogen (see *Dogen*).

Shunyata [Sanskrit]: emptiness; a key concept in Buddhism, referring to the impermanent, nonessential, interdependent nature of all things, so that no one thing exists in itself; often contrasted with form, the apparent existence of things; in many schools of Mahayana (including Zen) and Vajrayana Buddhism, synonymous with nirvana or the nondual absolute.

Siddhartha [Sanskrit]: literally, "all is fulfilled"; the first name of the historical Buddha.

Six worlds (or realms): in many schools of Mahayana (including Zen) and Vajrayana Buddhism, the various forms of life into which one can be reborn (or, symbolically, the various forms of life in which one can dwell mentally, emotionally, or spiritually). In most schools they are, in ascending order based on comfort, the realms inhabited by (1) demons, (2) hungry ghosts, (3) animals, (4) fighting demons; (5) humans, and (6) gods. In some schools, there is no realm of fighting demons but, instead, a realm of demigods between the realms of humans and gods. Other schools only recognize five realms, excluding any realm of fighting demons or demigods. The six worlds are mentioned in the meal gatha at Zen Mountain Monastery (see p. 175).

Skandhas [Sanskrit]: the five conditions or aggregates that collectively make up a person's identity or personality, even though no such thing as a separate "self" exists: (1) matter, (2) sensations, (3) perception, (4) mental formation, and (5) consciousness. The skandhas or "five conditions" are mentioned in the *Heart Sutra* (see p. 173).

Sosan: a formal talk by a teacher or senior student (who is called, in this context, *sosanji*), followed by a formal question-and-answer "challenge" session featuring individual students, in the manner of a public dokusan (see *Dokusan*); sometimes referred to as dharma combat.

Soto: one of the main schools of Zen, imported from China by Dogen in the thirteenth century and centering around the practice of shikantaza, or meditation, without any added technique such as koan study.

Stupa [Sanskrit]: a Buddhist architectural style used mainly for reliquaries, memorials, or monuments; in India, southeast Asia, and Tibet, typically dome- or pedestal-shaped with a central spire; in China, Korea, and Japan, typically pagoda-shaped with multiple stories.

Sutra [Sanskrit]: Buddhist scripture that is presumed to represent the Buddha's teachings in his own words.

Tathagata [Sanskrit]: literally, "thus-perfected one"; one of the Buddha's titles.

Tathata [Sanskrit]: literally, "thusness" or "suchness"; key concept of Mahayana (including Zen) and Vajrayana Buddhism, referring to the absolute nature of all things and, accordingly, each thing.

Teisho: a formal commentary by a Zen master on a Zen text; also called a dharma discourse.

Ten directions: symbolic phrase for the whole cosmos: the four main directions plus the four intermediate directions and the zenith and nadir.

Ten Ox-Herding Pictures: an ancient Ch'an (and, later, Zen) teaching device, using drawings of an ox-herder and (in most of the pictures) his ox to symbolize the ten stages on the path to enlightenment. In some schools, only eight pictures are involved.

Ten thousand things: symbolic phrase for all the phenomena in the universe.

Tenzo: the chief cook at a Zen monastery, traditionally a very important office, often held by a senior monk or roshi.

Three pillars: refers to the essential components of Zen practice: great doubt, great faith, great determination.

Three poisons: greed, anger, and ignorance: the characteristics of a deluded being; an enlightened being is characterized by the opposing qualities of compassion, wisdom, and enlightenment.

Three treasures [in Sanskrit, *triratna*]: the core elements in all schools of Buddhism: the Buddha, the dharma, and the sangha; also known as the three jewels.

Three vehicles [in Sanskrit, *triyana*]: different embodiments of doctrine that can bring one to enlightenment; in the *Lotus Sutra*, identified as (1) Theravada, (2) Mahayana, and (3) Pratyeka, or "middle vehicle," leading directly to buddhahood without the arhat or bodhisattva stage; in more recent times, identified as (1) Theravada, (2) Mahayana, and (3) Vajrayana, which differs from Pratyeka.

Tokodu: in Zen, the ceremony of receiving the precepts; most commonly used in reference to the ordination of a monk or nun.

Torii: the traditional Japanese gateway consisting of two upright posts and a top cross post.

Trikaya [Sanskrit]: literally, "three bodies"; key concept in Mahayana (including Zen) and Vajrayana Buddhism, referring to the various manifestations of a buddha/bodhisattva: (1) *dharmakaya*, the truth or essence body, which is the absolute nature of the buddha; (2) *sambhogakaya*, the bliss or archetypal body, which is an emanation of certain aspects of a buddha/bodhisattva; and (3) *nirmanakaya*, the form body, which is the physical incarnation of a buddha/bodhisattva—the most recent one being Shakyamuni, the historical Buddha.

Upaya [Sanskrit]: skillful means; the most effective way, given the situation, to express the dharma or enact the precepts. Every Buddhist aspires to use skillful means at all times, but it's especially a characteristic of a bodhisattva.

Vipassana [Pali; in Sanskrit, Vipashyana]: insight, commonly associated with a form of meditation most prominent in Theravada Buddhism.

Zabuton: in Zen, the square mat on which a zafu (or meditation cushion) is placed.

Zafu: in Zen, the cushion on which one meditates.

Zazen: literally, "sitting meditation"; the Zen form of meditation, in which one simply sits and frees the mind from thoughts.

Zazenkai: a gathering of Zen practitioners; also a name given to a one-day sesshin (see *Sesshin*).

Zen [in Chinese, Ch'an]: literally, "meditation"; one of the main schools of Buddhism in Japan, carried over from the Chinese Ch'an school beginning in the thirteenth century. It emphasizes meditation over all other practices as a means of achieving enlightenment within one's lifetime.

Zendo: large hall or room in which zazen is practiced.

Zenji: great or renowned master: a title usually bestowed posthumously, for example, Dogen Zenji (see *Dogen*).

Notes

Notes

Notes

About SKYLIGHT PATHS Publishing

SkyLight Paths Publishing is creating a place where people of different spiritual traditions come together for challenge and inspiration, a place where we can help each other understand the mystery that lies at the heart of our existence.

Through spirituality, our religious beliefs are increasingly becoming a part of our lives—rather than *apart* from our lives. While many of us may be more interested than ever in spiritual growth, we may be less firmly planted in traditional religion. Yet, we do want to deepen our relationship to the sacred, to learn from our own as well as from other faith traditions, and to practice in new ways.

SkyLight Paths sees both believers and seekers as a community that increasingly transcends traditional boundaries of religion and denomination—people wanting to learn from each other, *walking together, finding the way.*

We at SkyLight Paths take great care to produce beautiful books that present meaningful spiritual content in a form that reflects the art of making high quality books. Therefore, we want to acknowledge those who contributed to the production of this book.

PRODUCTION
Marian B. Wallace & Bridgett Taylor

EDITORIAL
David O'Neal & Emily Wichland

COVER DESIGN
Bronwen Battaglia, Scituate, Massachusetts

TEXT DESIGN
Chelsea Cloeter, Scotia, New York

PRINTING & BINDING
Lake Book, Melrose Park, Illinois

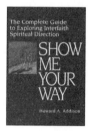  

Spirituality

Who Is My God?
An Innovative Guide to Finding Your Spiritual Identity
Created by *the Editors at SkyLight Paths*

Spiritual Type™ + Tradition Indicator = Spiritual Identity

Your Spiritual Identity is an undeniable part of who you are—whether you've thought much about it or not. This dynamic resource provides a helpful framework to begin or deepen your spiritual growth. Start by taking the unique Spiritual Identity Self-Test™; tabulate your results; then explore one, two or more of twenty-eight faiths/spiritual paths followed in America today. "An innovative and entertaining way to think—and rethink—about your own spiritual path, or perhaps even to find one." —*Dan Wakefield*, author of *How Do We Know When It's God?*
6 x 9, 160 pp, Quality PB Original, ISBN 1-893361-08-X **$15.95**

Spiritual Manifestos: *Visions for Renewed Religious Life in America from Young Spiritual Leaders of Many Faiths*
Edited by *Niles Elliot Goldstein*; Preface by *Martin E. Marty*

Discover the reasons why so many people have kept organized religion at arm's length.

Here, ten young spiritual leaders, most in their mid-thirties, representing the spectrum of religious traditions—Protestant, Catholic, Jewish, Buddhist, Unitarian Universalist—present the innovative ways they are transforming our spiritual communities and our lives. "These ten articulate young spiritual leaders engender hope for the vitality of 21st-century religion." —*Forrest Church*, Minister of All Souls Church in New York City
6 x 9, 256 pp, HC, ISBN 1-893361-09-8 **$21.95**

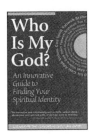

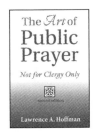

The Art of Public Prayer: *Not for Clergy Only,* 2nd Edition
by *Lawrence A. Hoffman*

A resource for worshipers today looking to change hardened worship patterns that stand in the way of everyday spirituality.

Written for laypeople and clergy of any denomination, this ecumenical introduction to meaningful public prayer is for everyone who cares about religion today.
6 x 9, 288 pp, Quality PB, ISBN 1-893361-06-3 **$17.95**

Spirituality

Three Gates to Meditation Practice
A Personal Journey into Sufism, Buddhism, and Judaism
by *David A. Cooper*

Shows us how practicing within more than one spiritual tradition can lead us to our true home.

Here are over fifteen years from the journey of "post-denominational rabbi" David A. Cooper, author of *God Is a Verb*, and his wife, Shoshana—years in which the Coopers explored a rich variety of practices, from chanting Sufi *dhikr* to Buddhist Vipassanā meditation, to the study of kabbalah and esoteric Judaism. Their experience demonstrates that the spiritual path is really completely within our reach, whoever we are, whatever we do—as long as we are willing to practice it. 5½ x 8½, 240 pp, Quality PB, ISBN 1-893361-22-5 **$16.95**

Praying with Our Hands: *Twenty-One Practices of Embodied Prayer from the World's Spiritual Traditions*
by *Jon M. Sweeney*; Photographs by *Jennifer J. Wilson*;
Foreword by *Mother Tessa Bielecki*; Afterword by *Taitetsu Unno, Ph.D.*

A spiritual guidebook for bringing prayer into our bodies.

What gives our prayers meaning? How can we carry a prayerful spirit throughout our everyday lives? This inspiring book of reflections and accompanying photographs shows us twenty-one simple ways of using our hands to speak to God, to enrich our devotion and ritual. All express the various approaches of the world's religious traditions to bringing the body into worship. Spiritual traditions represented include Anglican, Sufi, Zen, Roman Catholic, Yoga, Shaker, Hindu, Jewish, Pentecostal, Eastern Orthodox, and many others. 8 x 8, 96 pp, 22 duotone photographs, Quality PB Original, ISBN 1-893361-16-0 **$16.95**

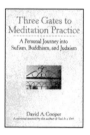
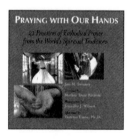
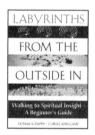

Labyrinths from the Outside In
Walking to Spiritual Insight—a Beginner's Guide
by *Donna Schaper & Carole Ann Camp*

The user-friendly, interfaith guide to making and using labyrinths— for meditation, prayer, and celebration.

Labyrinth walking is a spiritual exercise *anyone* can do. And it's rare among such practices in that it can be done by people together, regardless of their religious backgrounds or lack thereof. This accessible guide unlocks the mysteries of the labyrinth for all of us, providing ideas for using the labyrinth walk for prayer, meditation, and celebrations to mark the most important moments in life. Includes instructions for making a labyrinth of your own and finding one in your area. 6 x 9, 208 pp, b/w illus. and photographs, Quality PB Original, ISBN 1-893361-18-7 **$16.95**

Spirituality

One God Clapping: *The Spiritual Path of a Zen Rabbi*

by *Alan Lew & Sherril Jaffe*

The firsthand account of a spiritual journey from Zen Buddhist practitioner to rabbi.

A fascinating personal story of a Jewish meditation expert's roundabout spiritual journey from Zen Buddhist practitioner to rabbi. An insightful source of inspiration for each of us who is on the journey to find God in today's multi-faceted spiritual world. 5½ x 8½, 336 pp, Quality PB, ISBN 1-58023-115-2 **$16.95** (Available Feb. 2001)

Zen Effects: *The Life of Alan Watts*

by *Monica Furlong*

The first and only full-length biography of one of the most charismatic spiritual leaders of the twentieth century—now back in print!

Through his widely popular books and lectures, Alan Watts (1915–1973) did more to introduce Eastern philosophy and religion to Western minds than any figure before or since. Here is the only biography of this charismatic figure, who served as Zen teacher, Anglican priest, lecturer, academic, entertainer, a leader of the San Francisco renaissance, and author of more than 30 books, including *The Way of Zen, Psychotherapy East and West* and *The Spirit of Zen.* 6 x 9, 272 pp, Quality PB, ISBN 1-893361-32-2 **$16.95** (Available Feb. 2001)

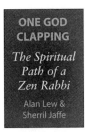  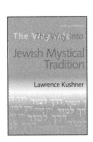 

The Way Into Jewish Mystical Tradition

by *Lawrence Kushner*

Explains the principles of Jewish mystical thinking, their religious and spiritual significance, and how they relate to our lives. A book that allows us to experience and understand the Jewish mystical approach to our place in the world. 6 x 9, 176 pp, HC, ISBN 1-58023-029-6 **$21.95**

The New Millennium Spiritual Journey
Change Your Life—Develop Your Spiritual Priorities with Help from Today's Most Inspiring Spiritual Teachers

Created by *the Editors at SkyLight Paths*

A life-changing resource for reimagining your spiritual life.

Set your own course of reflection and spiritual transformation with the help of self-tests, spirituality exercises, sacred texts from many traditions, time capsule pages, and helpful suggestions from more than 20 spiritual teachers, including Karen Armstrong, Sylvia Boorstein and Dr. Andrew Weil. 7 x 9, 144 pp, Quality PB Original, ISBN 1-893361-05-5 **$16.95**

Spirituality

Honey from the Rock
An Introduction to Jewish Mysticism
by *Lawrence Kushner*

An insightful and absorbing introduction to the ten gates of Jewish mysticism and how it applies to daily life. "The easiest introduction to Jewish mysticism you can read."
6 x 9, 176 pp, Quality PB, ISBN 1-58023-073-3 **$15.95**

Eyes Remade for Wonder
The Way of Jewish Mysticism and Sacred Living
A Lawrence Kushner Reader

Intro. by *Thomas Moore*, author of *Care of the Soul*

Whether you are new to Kushner or a devoted fan, you'll find inspiration here. With samplings from each of Kushner's works, and a generous amount of new material, this book is to be read and reread, each time discovering deeper layers of meaning in our lives.
6 x 9, 240 pp, Quality PB, ISBN 1-58023-042-3 **$16.95**; HC, ISBN 1-58023-014-8 **$23.95**

Invisible Lines of Connection
Sacred Stories of the Ordinary
by *Lawrence Kushner* AWARD WINNER!

Through his everyday encounters with family, friends, colleagues and strangers, Kushner takes us deeply into our lives, finding flashes of spiritual insight in the process.
5½ x 8½, 160 pp, Quality PB, ISBN 1-879045-98-2 **$15.95**; HC, ISBN 1-879045-52-4 **$21.95**

Finding Joy
A Practical Spiritual Guide to Happiness
by *Dannel I. Schwartz* with *Mark Hass* AWARD WINNER!

Explains how to find joy through a time-honored, creative—and surprisingly practical—approach based on the teachings of Jewish mysticism and Kabbalah.
6 x 9, 192 pp, Quality PB, ISBN 1-58023-009-1 **$14.95**; HC, ISBN 1-879045-53-2 **$19.95**

Ancient Secrets
Using the Stories of the Bible to Improve Our Everyday Lives
by *Rabbi Levi Meier, Ph.D.* AWARD WINNER!

Drawing on a broad range of wisdom writings, distinguished rabbi and psychologist Levi Meier takes a thoughtful, wise and fresh approach to showing us how to apply the stories of the Bible to our everyday lives.
5½ x 8½, 288 pp, Quality PB, ISBN 1-58023-064-4 **$16.95**

Spirituality

Does the Soul Survive? *A Jewish Journey to Belief in Afterlife, Past Lives & Living with Purpose*

by *Rabbi Elie Kaplan Spitz;*

Foreword by *Brian L. Weiss, M.D., author of* Many Lives, Many Masters

Some surprising answers to what Judaism teaches us about life after life.

Do we have a soul that survives our earthly existence? To know the answer is to find greater understanding, comfort and purpose in our lives—and in our deaths. Here, Rabbi Elie Kaplan Spitz relates his own experiences and those shared with him by people he has worked with as a rabbi, firsthand accounts that helped propel his own journey from skeptic to believer. Spitz shows us that beliefs in these concepts, so often approached with reluctance, is in fact true to Jewish tradition. 6 x 9, 240 pp, HC, ISBN 1-58023-094-6 **$21.95**

Bringing the Psalms to Life
How to Understand and Use the Book of Psalms by *Rabbi Daniel F. Polish*

Here, the most beloved—and least understood—of the books in the Bible comes alive. This simultaneously insightful and practical guide shows how the psalms address a myriad of spiritual issues in our lives: feeling abandoned, overcoming illness, dealing with anger, and more. 6 x 9, 208 pp, HC, ISBN 1-58023-077-6 **$21.95**

The Way of Flame
A Guide to the Forgotten Mystical Tradition of Jewish Meditation

by *Avram Davis* 4½ x 8, 176 pp, Quality PB, ISBN 1-58023-060-1 **$15.95**

  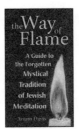 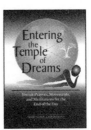 

Minding the Temple of the Soul: *Balancing Body, Mind, and Spirit through Traditional Jewish Prayer, Movement, and Meditation*

by *Tamar Frankiel* and *Judy Greenfeld*

This new spiritual approach to physical health introduces us to practices that affirm the body and enable us to reconceive our bodies in a more positive spiritual light. Focuses on traditional Jewish prayers and Kabbalah, with exercises, movements, and meditations. 7 x 10, 192 pp, Quality PB, Illus., ISBN 1-879045-64-8 **$16.95**; Audiotape of the Blessings, Movements and Meditations (60-min. cassette), JN01 **$9.95**; Videotape of the Movements and Meditations (46-min. VHS), S507 **$20.00**

Entering the Temple of Dreams: *Jewish Prayers, Movements, and Meditations for the End of the Day*

by *Tamar Frankiel* and *Judy Greenfeld*

Nighttime spirituality is much more than bedtime prayers! Here, you'll learn to combine prayer with movements and meditations to enhance your physical and psychological well-being before sleep. 7 x 10, 192 pp, Illus., Quality PB, ISBN 1-58023-079-2 **$16.95**

Spirituality

A Heart of Stillness
A Complete Guide to Learning the Art of Meditation
by *David A. Cooper*

The only complete, nonsectarian guide to meditation, from one of our most respected spiritual teachers.

Experience what mystics have experienced for thousands of years. *A Heart of Stillness* helps you acquire on your own, with minimal guidance, the skills of various styles of meditation. Draws upon the wisdom teachings of Christianity, Judaism, Buddhism, Hinduism, and Islam as it teaches you the processes of purification, concentration, and mastery in detail.
5½ x 8½, 272 pp, Quality PB, ISBN 1-893361-03-9 **$16.95**

Silence, Simplicity & Solitude
A Complete Guide to Spiritual Retreat at Home
by *David A. Cooper*

The classic personal spiritual retreat guide that enables readers to create their own self-guided spiritual retreat at home.

Award-winning author David Cooper traces personal mystical retreat in all of the world's major traditions, describing the varieties of spiritual practices for modern spiritual seekers. Cooper shares the techniques and practices that encompass the personal spiritual retreat experience, allowing readers to enhance their meditation practices and create an effective, self-guided spiritual retreat in their own homes—without the instruction of a meditation teacher. 5½ x 8½, 336 pp, Quality PB, ISBN 1-893361-04-7 **$16.95**

  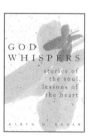  

God Whispers: *Stories of the Soul, Lessons of the Heart*
by Rabbi Karyn D. Kedar 6 x 9, 176 pp, Quality PB, ISBN 1-58023-088-1 **$15.95**

The Empty Chair: *Finding Hope and Joy—*
Timeless Wisdom from a Hasidic Master, Rebbe Nachman of Breslov AWARD WINNER!
Adapted by Moshe Mykoff and the Breslov Research Institute
4 x 6, 128 pp, Deluxe PB, 2-color text, ISBN 1-879045-67-2 **$9.95**

The Gentle Weapon: *Prayers for Everyday and Not-So-Everyday Moments*
Adapted from the Wisdom of Rebbe Nachman of Breslov by Moshe Mykoff and
S. C. Mizrahi, with the Breslov Research Institute
4 x 6, 144 pp, Deluxe PB, 2-color text, ISBN 1-58023-022-9 **$9.95**

Children's Spirituality

Becoming Me: *A Story of Creation*
by *Martin Boroson*
Full-color illus. by *Christopher Gilvan-Cartwright*

NONDENOMINATIONAL, NONSECTARIAN

For ages 4 & up

Told in the personal "voice" of the Creator, here is a story about creation and relationship that is about each one of us. In simple words and with radiant illustrations, the Creator tells an intimate story about love, about friendship and playing, about our world—and about ourselves. And with each turn of the page, we're reminded that we just might be closer to our Creator than we think!

8 x 10, 32 pp, Full-color illus., HC, ISBN 1-893361-11-X **$16.95**

A Prayer for the Earth
The Story of Naamah, Noah's Wife
by *Sandy Eisenberg Sasso*
Full-color illus. by *Bethanne Andersen*

NONDENOMINATIONAL, NONSECTARIAN

For ages 4 & up

This new story, based on an ancient text, opens children's religious imaginations to new ideas about the well-known story of the Flood. When God tells Noah to bring the animals of the world onto the ark, God also calls on Naamah, Noah's wife, to save each plant on Earth. "A lovely tale. . . . Children of all ages should be drawn to this parable for our times."
—*Tomie de Paola,* artist/author of books for children
9 x 12, 32 pp, HC, Full-color illus., ISBN 1-879045-60-5 **$16.95**

The 11th Commandment
Wisdom from Our Children
by *The Children of America*

For all ages

MULTICULTURAL, NONDENOMINATIONAL, NONSECTARIAN

"If there were an Eleventh Commandment, what would it be?" Children of many religious denominations across America answer this question—in their own drawings and words. From "No polluting the world," to "You shall not make fun of the handicapped," to "No punching in the head," this book helps us take a fresh look at how we can create a better world to live in. "A rare book of spiritual celebration for all people, of all ages, for all time."—Bookviews
8 x 10, 48 pp, HC, Full-color illus., ISBN 1-879045-46-X **$16.95**

Children's Spirituality

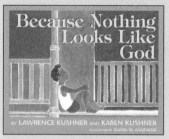

Because Nothing Looks Like God

by *Lawrence and Karen Kushner*
Full-color illus. by
Dawn W. Majewski

For ages 4 & up

A vibrant way for children— and their adults— to explore what, where, and how God is in our lives.

MULTICULTURAL, NONDENOMINATIONAL, NONSECTARIAN

What is God like? The first collaborative work by husband-and-wife team Lawrence and Karen Kushner introduces children to the possibilities of spiritual life with three poetic spiritual stories. Real-life examples of happiness and sadness—from goodnight stories, to the hope and fear felt the first time at bat, to the closing moments of life—invite us to explore, together with our children, the questions we all have about God, no matter what our age. 11 x 8½, 32 pp, HC, Full-color illus., ISBN 1-58023-092-X **$16.95**

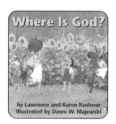

Where Is God? (A Board Book)

by *Lawrence and Karen Kushner*; Full-color illus. by *Dawn W. Majewski*

For ages 0–4

A gentle way for young children to explore how God is with us every day, in every way.

To young children the world is full of things to see and touch. This enchanting book gently invites children to become aware of God's presence all around them. Abridged from *Because Nothing Looks Like God* by Lawrence and Karen Kushner, *Where Is God?* has been specially adapted to board book format to delight and inspire young readers. 5 x 5, 24 pp, Board, Full-color illus., ISBN 1-893361-17-9 **$7.95**

What Is God's Name? (A Board Book)

Everyone and everything in the world has a name. What is God's name?

For ages 0–4

by *Sandy Eisenberg Sasso*; Full-color illus. by *Phoebe Stone*

Each child begins to formulate an image for God in their preschool years, often one dominant image they keep for a lifetime…"shepherd," "mother," "father," "friend." In this simple, beautiful abridged version of Sasso's award-winning *In God's Name*, children see and hear the many names people have for God, and learn that each name is equal to the others and that God is One. 5 x 5, 24 pp, Board, Full-color illus., ISBN 1-893361-10-1 **$7.95**

Children's Spirituality

In Our Image
God's First Creatures
by *Nancy Sohn Swartz*

Full-color illus. by *Melanie Hall*

For ages 4 & up

A playful new twist on the Creation story—from the perspective of the animals. Celebrates the interconnectedness of nature and the harmony of all living things. "The vibrantly colored illustrations nearly leap off the page in this delightful interpretation." —*School Library Journal*

"A message all children should hear, presented in words and pictures that children will find irresistible." —*Rabbi Harold Kushner*, author of *When Bad Things Happen to Good People*

9 x 12, 32 pp, HC, Full-color illus., ISBN 1-879045-99-0 **$16.95**

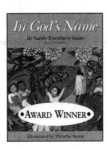

God's Paintbrush
by *Sandy Eisenberg Sasso*; Full-color illus. by *Annette Compton*

For ages 4 & up

Invites children of all faiths and backgrounds to encounter God openly in their own lives. Wonderfully interactive; provides questions adult and child can explore together at the end of each episode. "An excellent way to honor the imaginative breadth and depth of the spiritual life of the young." —*Dr. Robert Coles*, Harvard University

11 x 8½, 32 pp, HC, Full-color illus., ISBN 1-879045-22-2 **$16.95**

Also available: **A Teacher's Guide**
8½ x 11, 32 pp, PB, ISBN 1-879045-57-5 **$6.95**

God's Paintbrush Celebration Kit 9½ x 12, HC, Includes 5 sessions/40 full-color Activity Sheets and Teacher Folder with complete instructions, ISBN 1-58023-050-4 **$21.95**

In God's Name
by *Sandy Eisenberg Sasso*; Full-color illus. by *Phoebe Stone*

For ages 4 & up

Like an ancient myth in its poetic text and vibrant illustrations, this award-winning modern fable about the search for God's name celebrates the diversity and, at the same time, the unity of all the people of the world. "What a lovely, healing book!" —*Madeleine L'Engle*

9 x 12, 32 pp, HC, Full-color illus., ISBN 1-879045-26-5 **$16.95**

Children's Spirituality

God Said Amen

For ages
4 & up

by *Sandy Eisenberg Sasso*

Full-color illus. by *Avi Katz*

MULTICULTURAL, NONDENOMINATIONAL, NONSECTARIAN

A warm and inspiring tale of two kingdoms: Midnight Kingdom is overflowing with water but has no oil to light its lamps; Desert Kingdom is blessed with oil but has no water to grow its gardens. The kingdoms' rulers ask God for help but are too stubborn to ask each other. It takes a minstrel, a pair of royal riding-birds and their young keepers, and a simple act of kindness to show that they need only reach out to each other to find the answers to their prayers.

9 x 12, 32 pp, HC, Full-color illus., ISBN 1-58023-080-6 **$16.95**

For Heaven's Sake

For ages
4 & up

by *Sandy Eisenberg Sasso*; Full-color illus. by *Kathryn Kunz Finney*

Everyone talked about heaven: "Thank heavens." "Heaven forbid." "For heaven's sake, Isaiah." But no one would say what heaven was or how to find it. So Isaiah decides to find out, by seeking answers from many different people. "This book is a reminder of how well Sandy Sasso knows the minds of children. But it may surprise—and delight—readers to find how well she knows us grown-ups too." —*Maria Harris*, National Consultant in Religious Education, and author of *Teaching and Religious Imagination*
9 x 12, 32 pp, HC, Full-color illus., ISBN 1-58023-054-7 **$16.95**

But God Remembered

For ages
8 & up

Stories of Women from Creation to the Promised Land

by *Sandy Eisenberg Sasso*; Full-color illus. by *Bethanne Andersen*

A fascinating collection of four different stories of women only briefly mentioned in biblical tradition and religious texts. Award-winning author Sasso vibrantly brings to life courageous and strong women from ancient tradition; all teach important values through their actions and faith. "Exquisite. . . . A book of beauty, strength and spirituality." —*Association of Bible Teachers* 9 x 12, 32 pp, HC, Full-color illus., ISBN 1-879045-43-5 **$16.95**

God in Between

For ages
4 & up

by *Sandy Eisenberg Sasso*; Full-color illus. by *Sally Sweetland*

If you wanted to find God, where would you look? A magical, mythical tale that teaches that God can be found where we are: within all of us and the relationships between us. "This happy and wondrous book takes our children on a sweet and holy journey into God's presence." —*Rabbi Wayne Dosick, Ph.D.*, author of *The Business Bible* and *Soul Judaism*
9 x 12, 32 pp, HC, Full-color illus., ISBN 1-879045-86-9 **$16.95**

Spirituality

One God Clapping: *The Spiritual Path of a Zen Rabbi*

by *Alan Lew & Sherril Jaffe*

The firsthand account of a spiritual journey from Zen Buddhist practitioner to rabbi.

A fascinating personal story of a Jewish meditation expert's roundabout spiritual journey from Zen Buddhist practitioner to rabbi. An insightful source of inspiration for each of us who is on the journey to find God in today's multi-faceted spiritual world. 5½ x 8½, 336 pp, Quality PB, ISBN 1-58023-115-2 **$16.95** (Available Feb. 2001)

Zen Effects: *The Life of Alan Watts*

by *Monica Furlong*

The first and only full-length biography of one of the most charismatic spiritual leaders of the twentieth century—now back in print!

Through his widely popular books and lectures, Alan Watts (1915–1973) did more to introduce Eastern philosophy and religion to Western minds than any figure before or since. Here is the only biography of this charismatic figure, who served as Zen teacher, Anglican priest, lecturer, academic, entertainer, a leader of the San Francisco renaissance, and author of more than 30 books, including *The Way of Zen, Psychotherapy East and West* and *The Spirit of Zen.* 6 x 9, 272 pp, Quality PB, ISBN 1-893361-32-2 **$16.95** (Available Feb. 2001)

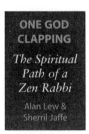  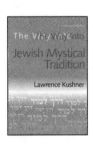 

The Way Into Jewish Mystical Tradition

by *Lawrence Kushner*

Explains the principles of Jewish mystical thinking, their religious and spiritual significance, and how they relate to our lives. A book that allows us to experience and understand the Jewish mystical approach to our place in the world. 6 x 9, 176 pp, HC, ISBN 1-58023-029-6 **$21.95**

The New Millennium Spiritual Journey
Change Your Life—Develop Your Spiritual Priorities with Help from Today's Most Inspiring Spiritual Teachers

Created by *the Editors at SkyLight Paths*

A life-changing resource for reimagining your spiritual life.

Set your own course of reflection and spiritual transformation with the help of self-tests, spirituality exercises, sacred texts from many traditions, time capsule pages, and helpful suggestions from more than 20 spiritual teachers, including Karen Armstrong, Sylvia Boorstein and Dr. Andrew Weil. 7 x 9, 144 pp, Quality PB Original, ISBN 1-893361-05-5 **$16.95**